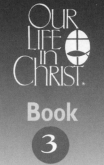

OUR
LIFE
in
CHRIST.

Book
3

Adult
Bible Studies

By Roger Sonnenberg

CPH
SAINT LOUIS

D0109950

Portions of the "Inform" and "Connect" sections were written by Kenneth Wagener.

This publication is also available in braille and in large print for the visually impaired. Write to the Library for the Blind, 1333 S. Kirkwood Rd., St. Louis, MO 63122-7295; or call 1-800-433-3954.

Quotations from the Small Catechism are from Luther's Small Catechism with Explanation, copyright © 1986, 1991 by Concordia Publishing House. All rights reserved.

Unless otherwise indicated, Scripture quotations are taken from the HOLY BIBLE: NEW INTERNATIONAL VERSION®. NIV®. Copyright © 1973, 1978, 1984 by International Bible Society. Used by permission of Zondervan Publishing House. All rights reserved.

Scripture quotations marked KJV are from the King James or Authorized Version of the Bible.

Copyright © 1997, 2000 Concordia Publishing House
3558 South Jefferson Avenue, St. Louis, MO 63118-3968
Manufactured in the United States of America

1   2   3   4   5   6   7   8   9   10   06   05   04   03   02   01

Contents

Introduction   5

Study Guide   7

Session   1: Jesus Provides for Us   9
(Matthew 14:4–21; Luke 10:25–37)

Session   2: Jesus Gives Us the Lord's Supper   16
(Luke 22:7–38)

Session   3: Jesus Prays in Gethsemane   24
(Luke 22:39–46)

Session   4: Peter Denies Jesus   31
(Luke 22:24–35, 54–62; 15:1–3, 11–32)

Session   5: Pilate Condemns Jesus   38
(Luke 22:66–23:25)

Session   6: Jesus Is Put to Death   47
(Luke 23:26–56)

Session   7: Jesus Rises from the Dead   56
(Luke 24:1–11; Matthew 28:1–10; 1 Corinthians 15:1–11)

Session   8: Jesus Appears at the Sea of Galilee   65
(John 21)

Session   9: Saul Becomes a Christian   74
(Acts 9:1–20)

Session   10: Paul Begins His Ministry   82
(Acts 9:21–31; 13:1–33)

Session 11: Paul Preaches to Jews and Gentiles   90
(Acts 13:44–52; 16:1–5; 2 Timothy 1:5–7; 3:14–16)

Session 12: Paul Proclaims the Good News in Lystra,
Derbe, Macedonia, and Philippi   98
(Acts 14:8–23; 16:6–15)

Session 13: Paul Proclaims the Good News to a Jailer   107
(Acts 16:16–40)

Adult Leaders Guide   115

Introduction

God promises to strengthen our life in Christ as we study His Word. The Our Life in Christ Bible study series provides you resources to assist you in studying God's Word. The series gives you an opportunity to study in-depth some familiar and, possibly, not-so-familiar biblical accounts.

Each of the 9 Bible study books has 13 sessions that are divided into 4 easy-to-use sections.

Focus—section 1 of each session focuses the participants' attention on the key concept that will be discovered in the session.

Inform—section 2 of each session explores a portion of Scripture with the use of a commentary and questions that help the participants study the text.

Connect—section 3 of each session helps the participants apply to their lives both God's Law and Gospel revealed in the scriptural account.

Vision—section 4 of each session provides the participants with practical suggestions for taking the theme of the lesson out of the classroom and into the world.

Our Life in Christ is designed to assist both novice and expert Bible students with resources that will enable them to grow in their understanding of God's Word while strengthening their life in Christ.

As an added benefit, the sessions in the Our Life in Christ adult Bible study series follow the Scripture lessons taught in the Our Life in Christ Sunday school series. Parents will enjoy studying in-depth the Scripture lessons their children are studying in Sunday school. This will provide parents additional opportunities to discuss God's Word with their children.

We pray that as you study God's Word using the Our Life in Christ Bible study series your life in Christ may be strengthened.

Adult Study Guide

Session 1

Jesus Provides for Us

(Matthew 14:14–21; Luke 10:25–37)

Focus

Theme: Our Greatest Need

Law/Gospel Focus

Our human needs are great. At times because of sin we may focus our attention on providing for our physical needs while neglecting our greatest need—the need for forgiveness of sins and eternal life. In Christ, God forgives our selfish desires and sinful habits and provides for us that which will last into eternity—life. God's great love for us compels us to love God and our neighbor.

Objectives

By the power of the Holy Spirit working through God's Word, we will
1. describe how Jesus has provided for our greatest need;
2. explain what it means to love our neighbor;
3. seek new ways to love our neighbor and in so doing provide for his or her greatest need.

Opening Worship

Speak together the First Article of the Apostles' Creed and Luther's explanation.

I believe in God, the Father Almighty, Maker of heaven and earth.

What does this mean? I believe that God has made me and all creatures; that He has given me my body and soul, eyes, ears, and all my members, my reason and all my senses, and still takes care of them.

He also gives me clothing and shoes, food and drink, house and home, wife and children, land, animals, and all I have. He richly and daily provides me with all that I need to support this body and life.

He defends me against all danger and guards and protects me from all evil.

All this He does only out of fatherly, divine goodness and mercy, without any merit or worthiness in me. For all this it is my duty to thank and praise, serve and obey Him.

This is most certainly true.

Introduction

1. List needs you or others seek to have met.

2. How might our human needs and our striving to meet these needs at times get in the way of having our greatest need met—faith in the assurance of the forgiveness of sins and the eternal life Jesus won on the cross?

3. How might neglect of our spiritual need hamper our ability to love God and our neighbor?

In today's lesson we focus on how Jesus fulfills our needs and how we who have our greatest need fulfilled by God's grace through faith in Jesus can demonstrate His love to our neighbor.

Inform

Reading the Text

Read aloud Matthew 14:14–21 and Luke 10:25–37.

Matthew 14:14–21. As Jesus steps off the boat and onto land, He sees a great crowd with great needs. As a shepherd cares for his flock, so Jesus has "compassion" on God's people, feeding their souls with His words of life and healing their illnesses with His divine power.

As the day wears on, however, these men, women, and children also begin to experience physical hunger. The compassionate Savior does not "send the crowds away," as His disciples suggest (v. 15). He desires to satisfy their earthly needs, too.

Before feeding the crowd, however, Jesus tests the disciples: "You give them something to eat" (v. 16). The disciples fail the test. No one understands the nature of Jesus' instruction. No one recognizes that Jesus can and will provide.

"Loaves of bread" (v. 17) were large, round cakes, a few inches thick, made of wheat or barley. (The Gospel of John reports that Andrew discovered the boy among the crowd; the five loaves and two fish may have been the child's lunch.)

Jesus' command to the disciples, to have the people "sit down" (v. 19), was unusual. The word normally meant "to recline for the purpose of eating a meal." Will Jesus the host serve the boy's lunch to this multitude? Jesus looks reverently toward heaven, gives thanks, breaks the loaves, and distributes His gifts, first to the disciples and then through the disciples to the people. The meal outdoors is reminiscent of God's great provision to Israel during the wilderness wandering. The meal also anticipates another holy meal, the Lord's Supper, the giving of the Messiah's body and blood for the forgiveness of sins. (The Lord's Supper, of course, points forward to the messianic feast in heaven.)

"The disciples picked up twelve basketfuls of broken pieces" (v. 20). God's abundance is more than sufficient—for all Israel. (The number 12 is likely symbolic of the 12 tribes of Israel.) Everyone eats and is satisfied. The Messiah gives life to God's hungry people.

Luke 10:25–37:

The expert in the law who stands up to put Jesus to the test is a representative of the "wise and learned" from whom the things of God remain hidden (10:21). He demonstrates his knowledge of the Old Testament Scriptures by quoting Deuteronomy 6:5 concerning love to God

11

and Leviticus 19:18 about love for the neighbor. He gives the correct answer; Jesus directs him to do the law, to put it into practice (8:21). ...

[This law expert] feels the need to "justify himself" for asking a question which had such a simple answer, one he himself easily supplied. So the lawyer asks a further question seeking to demonstrate that loving your neighbor as yourself does call for a legal definition of the term "neighbor." Generally among the Jews the neighbor was defined as a fellow countryman, one of the same race.

The story which Jesus tells overturns such an understanding of the word "neighbor." ... [The] Samaritan, whom the lawyer would probably have excluded from his definition of "neighbor," shows himself as the one who fulfilled the command to love one another, in this case even an enemy.

The expert in the law had asked: "Who is my neighbor?" In the parable which Jesus tells this question is answered. But Jesus goes a step further with the question he now puts to the lawyer: "Which of these three ... was a neighbor?" For Jesus the real question is not who is my neighbor but how does one prove oneself a neighbor to others. ... Jesus makes this hated Samaritan a model for true neighborliness. The Samaritan is one of the "little children" to whom has been revealed the hidden wisdom of God. He sees beyond the racial divisions of this world to the will of God which bids us to love the neighbor whoever that neighbor might be. ... The early church saw in the Good Samaritan none other than Christ himself. No one else so radically fulfilled the love commandment. Faith in Jesus is the way to eternal life, a faith which shows its life by love for God and neighbor.

(From Victor H. Prange, *The People's Bible: Luke.* © 1988 Northwestern Publishing House. Used by permission. [Reprinted by CPH as *The People's Bible Commentary: Luke*, 1992, pp. 125–6.])

Discussing the Text

1. How does Jesus demonstrate His concern for people's physical needs? Why is this important for us to know?

2. How does the Messiah give spiritual life to God's hungry people?

3. How does Jesus provide for our needs in the spiritual meal He provides us—the Lord's Supper?

4. Consider the parable of the Good Samaritan. Who is your neighbor? How is this different than most people's conception of neighbor?

5. How does Jesus reveal Himself in the parable of the Good Samaritan as the true Good Samaritan?

Connect

Human needs are great. Every day we crave food and water for
basic sustenance. Our spiritual needs, however, are even greater. Too
often, though, we ignore the means to sustain and nourish our relationship with God. In truth, sin stands at the root of our neglect. We
are satisfied with "bread for the moment," and God seems remote
from our everyday cares and routines. Because the sinful nature
remains in all people, we do not—and cannot properly—"fear, love
and trust God above all things." In Christ, God forgives our selfish
desires and sinful habits. Jesus is the Father's gift to the world, a gift
that bestows life, hope, and eternal salvation through His death and
resurrection. As our Good Shepherd, Jesus feeds us with His Word,
with baptismal grace, and with His body and blood.

"Go and do likewise" (Luke 10:37). God's Law demands that we
love, support, and show compassion to all people. By nature, we cannot keep God's command; on our own we cannot be a "Good Samaritan." Jesus, the true "Good Samaritan," has fulfilled the Law's
demand in our place. His atoning sacrifice is our hope of forgiveness
and the source of strength to love both God and our neighbor as He
has loved us.

1. How do you often ignore or neglect the means God provides to sustain and to nourish your relationship to Him?

2. What does God continue to offer to you even as you fail to "fear, love, and trust God above all things"?

3. How might you better demonstrate love to your "neighbor"?

4. What motivates us to "Go and do likewise"?

5. Write a prayer of thanksgiving for all that God provides for you—physical and spiritual needs. Be prepared to share the prayer during closing worship.

Vision

Family Connection

1. Create a family list of the many blessings God provides for you.

2. Ask, "What greatest need do we have that God has provided for? How did Jesus provide for this greatest need?"

3. Discuss how your family might be better neighbors to those in need.

Personal Reflection

1. Think of a person to whom you could be a good Samaritan. Then be a good Samaritan to that person.

2. Make a list of all that God has provided to you. Then give thanks to Him for each of these blessings.

3. Develop a plan to spend more time in God's Word.

Closing Worship

Pray aloud the prayers of thanksgiving written earlier in this session.

For Next Week

Read Luke 22:7–38 in preparation for the next session.

Session 2

Jesus Gives Us the Lord's Supper

(Luke 22:7–38)

——— Focus ———

Theme: Dining at Its Best!

Law/Gospel Focus

We were dead spiritually; however, new life was provided for us through the life, death, and resurrection of Jesus Christ. By the power of the Holy Spirit working through the Word and Sacraments, He not only gave us this new life but continues to sustain and to strengthen it. In the Sacrament of Holy Communion God provides forgiveness of sins and eternal life.

Objectives

By the power of the Holy Spirit working through God's Word, we will

1. rejoice that God provides us with the Lord's Supper as a means of grace through which Christians receive forgiveness of sins, faith-strengthening power, and the assurance of eternal life;
2. thank God for the gift of grace and love that Jesus provides us through the Lord's Supper;
3. partake of the Lord's Supper often for strength and hope as we journey toward our heavenly home.

Opening Worship

Read responsively the following dialogue-prayer based on Luke 22:19–20.

Leader: Lord Jesus, on the night of Your betrayal, You poured Your love out to Your disciples and Your church as You gave the most intimate of meals—Your Supper—Holy Communion.

Participants: This is My body given *for you.*

Leader: What wondrous love! For "whoever believes … shall not perish but have eternal life" (John 3:16).

Participants: Through Your Holy Spirit we believe we have eternal life through Your life, death, and resurrection.

Leader: This cup is the new covenant in My blood, which is poured out *for you.*

Participants: What wondrous love! "Though your sins are like scarlet, they shall be as white as snow; though they are red as crimson, they shall be like wool" (Isaiah 1:18).

Leader: Through Your Holy Spirit we know and believe our sins are forgiven. Our thanks!

Participants: What wondrous love! You, O Lord, give us this special meal, that we might receive forgiveness of sins, faith-strengthening power, and the assurance of eternal life.

All: So strengthen us in this belief even now as we study Your Word. Amen.

Introduction

A story is told of a woman dying of a terminal illness. She calls her pastor, asking to talk to him about her funeral. "I would like John 14:1–6 read at my funeral," she tells the pastor. The pastor jots the information down on a notepad, assuring her it will be read. "As for hymns, I would like 'I'm But a Stranger Here' and 'Amazing Grace' sung." Again, the pastor notes the two hymns.

After sharing a few other details, the pastor thinks the woman has finished sharing her requests, and he gets ready to leave. "One more thing," the woman says, "could you please put into my one hand the Bible I love so much and into my other hand a silver fork from my silverware set?"

"I understand the Bible, but why the silver fork?" he asks.

"Because I remember when I was a child, during special times when we were invited out to someone's house for dinner, the hostess would sometimes come behind us and say, 'You may keep your fork,' as she gathered up the main plates. I knew this meant that the best was yet to come—the dessert. Not any ordinary dessert, but yummy homemade dessert—homemade apple pie or chocolate cake." The pastor jots it down with a smile on his face.

"Finally, Pastor, when people parade by my casket and they see the silver fork in my hand and ask why, tell them, because 'the best has come for me!'"

1. In what way is the Lord's Supper like the "dessert" in the worship service?

2. How does the Lord's Supper assure us "the best is yet to come"?

3. Sometimes pastors and church leaders feel they need to hurry with Holy Communion so that the service does not take too long. If we use the analogy of the Lord's Supper as dessert, how might we approach it differently?

Inform

Reading the Text

Read aloud Luke 22:7–38.

Passover is both the historical event—God's mighty rescue of His people from slavery in Egypt—and the religious festival that commemorates God's power and grace. Old Testament believers told and retold the story of God's salvation. Connected with the Festival of Unleavened Bread, "a lasting ordinance for the generations to come" (Exodus 12:17), it was a vivid, concrete way by which God's people rehearsed their redemption. In mercy, God provided a meal as a tangible reminder of His many past blessings. Gathered around the table, families began the celebration with a question, usually spoken by the youngest male: "Why do we celebrate this night?" The father, or oldest male, then responded by retelling the story.

Preparation for the sacred meal began on Thursday morning. Every particle of leaven—fermented dough—was destroyed. Afterward, the family joined in a ceremonial search of each room to ensure that no leaven remained anywhere in the house. When the Israelites fled Egypt, they left in haste and had no time to bake leavened bread (Exodus 12:34). Other typical Passover preparations included selecting the place where the meal would be eaten; setting the table with bowls of salt water and bitter herbs to represent the tears and bitterness of life as slaves in Egypt; mixing the *charoseth*, a paste of apples, dates, and nuts, as a reminder of the daily task of "mixing" clay and straw to make bricks for Pharaoh; and pouring the four cups of wine, reminders of God's promises to His people (Exodus 6:6–7).

As Master, Jesus authorizes the disciples to make preparations in His name. He entrusts Peter and John with the task of locating the guest room, "all furnished," where He will spend the evening in celebration of God's goodness and in fellowship with His friends. It is, to be sure, the night of His betrayal and arrest; on Friday, Jesus will stand trial and be condemned by both the religious and secular rulers. Yet the Lord Jesus knows the course of events before Him. His "appointed time" has drawn near (Matthew 26:18; see also John 13:1). His life's purpose, to suffer and die for the sins of all people, will soon be revealed to the world. He therefore journeys silently, willingly, toward Calvary.

Jesus has "eagerly desired" to eat the Passover with His disciples. He will not eat or drink this sacred meal again "until it finds fulfillment in the kingdom of God" (Luke 22:16). The Passover anticipates the holy meal that Jesus inaugurates: the Lord's Supper. For God's people, the church, the Lord's Supper *is* the fulfillment of God's purposes and blessings in the Passover. Christ, the true "Passover lamb" (1 Corinthians 5:7), will be sacrificed to spare us from judgment and give us life and salvation.

"I will not drink again of the fruit of the vine until the kingdom of God comes" (v. 18). Although He understood that He would be forsaken by His disciples and His Father, although He knew that death by crucifixion was only hours away, Jesus looked beyond the present moment to the kingdom of God. His words do not reflect a shallow optimism. Instead, Jesus had deep trust and knowledge that through His perfect obedience and willing sacrifice the kingdom of God would come to a world fractured by sin and hostility.

"He took bread … He took the cup" (vv. 19, 20). Jesus institutes His Supper. All four Gospel accounts, as well as Paul's witness to the Corinthian Christians (1 Corinthians 11:23–26), include a description of the Lord's actions and His words to the disciples. "This is My body. … This cup is the new covenant in My blood." Christ gives His body and His blood, sacrificed and shed on the cross "for the forgiveness of sins" (see Matthew 26:28). His Supper bestows, confirms, and seals forgiveness, life, and salvation for His disciples, who gather in His name and eat the bread—His body—and drink the wine—His blood.

Martin Luther once wrote, "I certainly love it with all my heart, the precious blessed Supper of my Lord Jesus Christ, in which He gives me His body and blood to eat and to drink, with the mouth of my body, accompanied by the exceedingly sweet and gracious words: Given for you, shed for you."

Discussing the Text

1. Compare and contrast the Passover celebrated by the Israelites in the Old Testament and the Christian celebration of the Lord's Supper described in the New Testament.
   a. Exodus 12:18/Luke 22:19

   b. Exodus 12:22/Luke 22:20/Matthew 26:28

   c. Exodus 12:23/Matthew 26:28

   d. Exodus 12:26/1 Corinthians 11:28

   e. Exodus 12:21/1 Corinthians 5:7

f. Exodus 12:31–32/Matthew 26:28

2. How was Luke 22:16 fulfilled (Isaiah 53:7; John 1:29; 1 Corinthians 5:7)?

3. How would you respond to a friend who asks, "What does Christ give us in this sacrament?" See Matthew 26:26, 28; 1 Corinthians 10:16.

Connect

The Lord's Supper reveals Jesus' love for His church. God instituted the Passover celebration as a yearly reminder of His power and grace in rescuing His chosen people, Israel. Jesus instituted His Supper for His disciples to remember *regularly* His gift of salvation. The Lord knows our human weakness. He knows that on our own, because of our sinful human nature, we quickly drift away from His Word. He understands our anxieties, fears, and occasional spiritual emptiness. In His Supper, Jesus is truly present. He gives His body and blood for our forgiveness and renewal in faith. As the Passover reminded the Israelites of God's grace, even more the Lord's Supper gives strength and hope to Christians on our pilgrimage to our heavenly home.

In the Lord's Supper the forgiveness won by Christ for the whole world is personal—for me! How often we hear the truth "Jesus died for all." Yet we easily are overcome by doubts, feelings of inadequacy, and isolation from God. Did He really die *for me*? Did He take on Himself *my sins*? Is He truly *my Savior*? Left alone, without the comfort and assurance of the Word and the Sacraments, we can fall into despair. The Lord's Supper brings forgiveness to us personally. The Lord's own words, "for you," are our assurance. As we eat and drink the body and blood of our Savior, we know and have full confidence that His salvation is ours and we are His!

1. "And when your children ask you, 'What does this ceremony mean to you?' then tell them …" (Exodus 12:26). Suppose your children came to you after church and asked, "Dad (Mom), when you took Holy Communion this morning, what did it mean to you?" How would you respond?

2. Compare and contrast the absolution at the beginning of the worship service with the forgiveness offered during Holy Communion (1 Corinthians 11:24).

3. What comfort and assurance does God provide you in His intimate meal?

4. Though Holy Communion is offered in most churches only after one is confirmed (usually around the ages of 12–14), would there be anything wrong with a church offering Holy Communion to younger children once they've been instructed in the meaning of this Sacrament? What are the key things communicants must know and believe before they partake of Holy Communion?

Vision

Family Connection

1. Write a personal testimony of what the Lord's Supper means to you and then share it with your family during devotional time or at another appropriate time.

2. Read and sing together some of the hymns used during the celebration of Holy Communion.

3. Compare a family meal to the Lord's Supper. How are they similar? different?

Personal Reflection

1. Write a special letter to someone who has lost a loved one. Comfort him/her with the picture of the heavenly banquet that she/he will someday enjoy with the loved one.

2. Reread the appointed Scripture lessons. Meditate on God's goodness provided to you through the Lord's Supper.

3. Share with a friend the joy you have in knowing that through Jesus your sins are forgiven.

Closing Worship

Sing or read aloud this stanza and the refrain from "I Come, O Savior, to Your Table" (*Lutheran Worship* 247).

Your body crucified, O Savior,
Your blood which once for me was shed,
These are my life and strength forever,
By them my hungry soul is fed.

Refrain
Lord, may Your body and Your blood
Be for my soul the highest good.

For Next Week

Read Luke 22:39–46 in preparation for next week's session.

Session 3

Jesus Prays in Gethsemane

(Luke 22:39–46)

Focus

Theme: Intimate Communication

Law/Gospel Focus

Sin separated people from God; however, God reconnected people to Him through the life, death, and resurrection of Jesus Christ. We can now approach Him confidently "so that we may receive mercy and find grace to help us in our time of need" (Hebrews 4:16). Whenever Jesus Christ was in great anguish, He would approach God the Father in prayer. In the Garden of Gethsemane before His betrayal and crucifixion, Jesus spoke with His Father. In doing so, God strengthened Him to endure the powers of sin, death, and the power of the devil.

Objectives

By the power of the Holy Spirit working through God's Word, we will

1. identify some physical, emotional, and spiritual needs we have;
2. rejoice that in our hour of deepest darkness we can approach God confidently for grace and mercy through Jesus Christ;
3. celebrate with thanksgiving that He gives us promised help.

Opening Worship

Read responsively the following dialogue-prayer based on Luke 22:39–46.

Leader: Lord God, we pray as Jesus warned the disciples, that we do "not fall into temptation,"
Participants: The temptation of our sinful selves, the devil, and the world.
Leader: Lord God, we pray as Jesus did that "not My will, but Yours be done,"
Participants: A will that often seems contrary to our will.
Leader: Lord God, we pray that we "get up and pray so that [we] will not fall into temptation."
Participants: Even now as we study Your Word, enable us to hear what You have to say to us.
Leader: Give us wisdom to know and humility to accept Your will,
Participants: And strength to do it.
All: Amen.

Introduction

Acts 20:7–12 records that a man by the name of Eutychus fell asleep in church and fell from an upstairs window. Have you ever fallen asleep in church? When? Why?

Today we will see how important it is for us to be awake to the temptations of our sinful self, the world, and Satan. We will be reminded that God speaks to us through His Word and gives us the great privilege of communicating with Him in prayer.

Inform

Reading the Text

Read aloud Luke 22:39–46.

Jesus often prayed. After long days of public preaching, after vigorous opposition to His teaching and healing ministry, the Lord frequently withdrew by Himself to spend time in prayer with His heavenly Father (Luke 6:12). Morning and evening, and whenever He felt the weight of others' expectations and demands, Jesus prayed. Now, before the agony of suffering, shame, and death, He again seeks the comfort and assurance of speaking—and listening—to God. Jesus leaves the Upper Room to pray.

With His disciples Jesus travels to Gethsemane, a well-known orchard on the western slope of the Mount of Olives near Jerusalem. *Gethsemane* means "olive press." When they arrive, Jesus calls to Himself Peter, James, and John, His most trusted followers, and invites them to share His burden in prayer. (See Matthew 26:37–38.) "My soul is overwhelmed with sorrow to the point of death. Stay here and keep watch with Me" (Matthew 26:38).

Jesus' anguish is real. As He anticipates both the isolation and pain ahead of Him, He recalls the fellowship He has shared with His disciples. They have witnessed His miraculous powers, His divine authority to heal the sick, to cast out demons, and to control the forces of nature. They have stood silently in awe as He provided bread for the hungry and comfort to the poor and lonely. They have watched Him speak words of forgiveness and hope to thousands of men, women, and children. Will they now watch with Him at His time of need?

The desire for companionship, comfort, and support reveals Jesus as truly human, the Savior God who is like His people in every way except for sin (Hebrews 4:15).

"Pray that you will not fall into temptation." At the beginning of His ministry, Jesus faced temptation from Satan (Luke 4:1–13). Now, as His earthly ministry draws to a conclusion, the Lord once more prepares for His battle with the powers of darkness. Satan has already entered Judas Iscariot, enticing him to betray Jesus to the religious authorities (Luke 22:3–6). Satan also stands ready to "sift" the disciples as wheat (Luke 22:31–32). As Satan once "tempted" Job with the loss of his family, home, and health, so now Satan desires to lead the disciples into spiritual ruin. Jesus' words, in effect, remind His followers of the constant struggle not simply against human opponents but against "the spiritual forces of evil in the heavenly realms" (Ephesians 6:12). Only when they are strong in faith and anchored in God's Word can disciples resist temptation.

Jesus went "about a stone's throw" away from His disciples (v. 41). In an utterly quiet moment, He prayed intensely to His heavenly Father to "take this cup from Me" (v. 42), to spare Him the suffering and shame of the cross. The "cup" is a symbol of God's wrath (Isaiah 51:17) and the Messiah's suffering (Matthew 20:22–23). Fully human, Jesus was fearful of the pain and rejection He would soon experience. Yet He did not refuse the cup before Him: as the Father's obedient Son, He prays, "Not My will, but Yours be done" (Luke 22:42).

"An angel ... strengthened Him" (v. 43). God's heavenly messengers supported Jesus at the beginning of His ministry (Matthew 4:11). In mercy, the Father sends His "ministering spirit" (Hebrews 1:14) to strengthen the Son in His time of agony and isolation. His sweat "like drops of blood" (v. 44) may refer to acute perspiration rolling down Jesus' face and dropping to the ground. Or it may refer to actual "sweat and blood," a rare occurrence in persons who suffer extreme anguish and/or physical strain. Jesus' anguish, as well as the physical strain of crucifixion, were indeed extreme.

Jesus returned to His disciples three times (Matthew 26:44), and each time He found Peter, James, and John asleep. He again urged them to "pray so that you will not fall into temptation" (Luke 22:46). But the hour of His betrayal had arrived. As Judas and the crowd approached, Jesus prepared to go quietly, willingly, to His death.

Discussing the Text

1. What lesson can we learn from this account about the times when we feel anxious and troubled? What did Jesus do in order to prepare for the trouble that lay ahead of Him? What were the results?

2. What does the "cup" refer to in Luke 22:42? Refer also to Matthew 20:22–23; 26:39; and Isaiah 51:17.

3. Why does Jesus pray for God's will to be done?

4. How did Jesus find the disciples each time He returned from praying (Luke 22:45)?
   a. If you knew a dear friend of yours was close to death, wouldn't you stay at his/her side until he/she died? Why would the closest friends of Jesus fall asleep on Him?

   b. Some people deal with extreme anxiety or difficult problems by going to sleep. Could the events the disciples had faced and would face cause them to sleep? Why or why not?

   c. We can usually tell when someone is exhausted. What signs are apparent when an individual or a congregation drifts into spiritual slumber?

Connect

The Lord's prayer in the garden is one of the supreme moments of spiritual struggle recorded in Scripture. Jesus, as true man, experienced the kind of fear and sorrow in the face of pain and hardship that is common to human beings. But He was also fully aware of the divine wrath that would be poured out on Him as He carried the sins of the world—our sins—through suffering and a brutal death. In intense agony, He prayed that He might be spared this cup of suffering. Yet He faithfully accepted the will of His Father and demonstrated His love for all people.

We sometimes struggle to understand how Peter, James, and John could fail to remain awake during their Master's suffering. But fatigue, coupled with sorrow and anxiety, often leads to tense, troubled sleep. Jesus' encouragement to His frail disciples, *pray,* speaks to disciples of all time. He knows our frailties, our faults, our tendency to drift into spiritual slumber. He gently invites us to trust Him and call on Him in prayer for every need. Jesus is our Good Shepherd, who watches over His weak and wandering sheep.

1. If your child or friend comes to you with a problem he/she is having in school or at work, what will praying with her/him communicate?

2. "Thy will be done." How easy or difficult is it for you to "mean it when you say it"? Why?

3. Jesus warned the disciples, "Get up and pray so that you will not fall into temptation" (Luke 22:46). Name some of the major temptations you and your family face regarding your faith. How does "pray" empower you to face these temptations?

4. What comfort does the anguish Jesus endured provide you (Hebrews 4:15–16)?

Vision

Family Connection

1. Survey each member of your immediate family. Ask what they are worried or anxious about. Post these worries on the refrigerator door and ask that each member, as he/she opens the refrigerator door, pray about one of these concerns, remembering Hebrews 4:15–16.

2. Agree to spend time each day praying with each other.

3. Discuss prayer at the dinner table. Why is it important?

Personal Reflection

1. Choose someone from the congregation who is going through a difficult time in his/her life (e.g., death of a loved one). Write or phone this person, reminding him/her of Jesus' love and your love. Ask if you can do anything to help. Pray with him or her.

2. Pray each day for the sick in your congregation.

Closing Worship

Pray together the following prayer:

Give us this week, O God:
Ears open to hear Your will;
Minds ready to accept Your will;
Wills ready to do Your will;
And, above all, hearts ready to answer to Your will;
Through Jesus Christ our Lord. Amen.

For Next Week

Read Luke 22:24–35, 54–62; 15:1–3, 11–32 in preparation for next week's session.

Session 4

Peter Denies Jesus

(Luke 22:24–35, 54–62; 15:1–3, 11–32)

Focus

Theme: Our Faithlessness, His Faithfulness

Law/Gospel Focus

Like Peter and the prodigal son, we are filled with pride and self-confidence. We have a natural tendency to do it our way, to follow our sinful desires. Jesus, however, forgives our stubborn pride. Though we are faithless, He is always faithful. Through His life, death, and resurrection He brings us back into relationship with God and with one another, giving us new life.

Objectives

By the power of the Holy Spirit working through God's Word, we will
1. confess that we are often filled with pride and self-confidence, just like Peter and the prodigal son;
2. rejoice that though we are faithless, He is faithful;
3. celebrate that in Christ we have full redemption from the curse of the Law.

Opening Worship

Read responsively the following dialogue-prayer based on Luke 22:24–25, 54–62; 15:1–3, 11–32.
Leader: Lord God, we say:
Participants: We'll never deny You, Lord, "[we are] ready to go with You to prison and to death."
Leader: The warning You gave Peter is ours as well: "Before the rooster crows today, you will deny Me three times."

Participants: We confess with our tears as Peter did, I have
sinned. I have failed to be faithful, just as You said. Forgive
me.

Leader: Like the prodigal son, we live at times like we do not
need You, Lord;

Participants: And our verdict is the same as it was for the prodigal son; we eat with the pigs and find ourselves hungry
inside.

Leader: But thanks be to You, O Lord. While we are still a long
way off, You see us and are filled with compassion for us;
You run to us, throw Your arms around us and kiss us.

Participants: Though we are faithless, You are always faithful.

All: Great is Your faithfulness and great is our praise and thanks
for it. Amen.

Introduction

A seminarian was telling his friends about his summer job. He
had worked in the north woods with loggers. "That had to be hard
in more ways than one," one of his classmates said. "Not only hard
physically, but also spiritually. Did you get a lot of kidding for being
a Christian and a seminarian?"

"Didn't have any problem at all," said the seminarian. "In fact,
they never caught on that I was a Christian or a seminarian."

1. Have your co-workers caught on to the fact you are a Chris-tian?
   Why is it so difficult at times for Christians to share their faith outside the walls of the church building?

2. Can you recall a time when you were embarrassed to let others
   know you were a Christian? Why?

In today's lesson Peter denies knowing Jesus. Before we ask in dismay, "How could he do this?" we must examine our own lives and confess that we too have denied our Lord. The truth—God in His love for us through Christ invites us to receive forgiveness for the times we have echoed Peter's words, "I don't know Him!"

Inform

Reading the Text

Read aloud Luke 22:24–35, 54–62; 15:1–3, 11–32.

At times, the disciples simply failed to understand their Lord's words and actions. After He instituted the Lord's Supper, Jesus rose from the table to wash their feet. Foot-washing was a menial task, usually given to servants and children. For Jesus, however, it was a gesture of humility and service, a demonstration of His sacrificial concern for His dear children. Though Lord of the universe, He showed His love by giving His body and blood for the forgiveness of sins and by providing an "example" of ministry in His name. Note the disciples' response: they argued among themselves, "Who is the greatest?" (Luke 22:24).

Jesus reverses the ways of the world. Greatness in the Kingdom is not measured by power and prestige but by humility, service, and sacrifice. Jesus, of course, is the model, the exemplar: "I am among you as one who serves" (Luke 22:27). His self-giving death on behalf of the world is the premier demonstration of the nature of the Kingdom: glory in and through the cross!

After deserting Jesus and running away from the temple police (Mark 14:50), Peter and John followed the flicker of torches back to the high priest. Peter, through John's influence, was admitted to the courtyard. His faith in Jesus, though stretched to the breaking point at Gethsemane, prompted him to follow the events from "a distance." Peter wanted to know the fate of his Teacher and Lord.

Ancient courtyards were often filled both day and night with people and activity. Since it was Passover, the gathering in the high priest's courtyard may have been especially large. On such a dark, chilly night, Peter may have expected to "blend in" with the crowd, to stand unobtrusively near the fire and wait for the word from the trial. Shortly after he sat down, though, Peter was confronted by a young girl, the doorkeeper, who perhaps recognized him from among the disciples (see John 18:16–17). Her question threatened to reveal Peter's identity. His denial, then, was emphatic: "I don't know Him" (Luke 22:57). To escape further notice, Peter again mingled with the crowd and later stepped out into the portico at the entrance of the courtyard. Here another woman accused him. With this second denial Peter fell deeper, for he confirmed it with an oath (see Matthew 26:72).

After "about an hour" (Luke 22:59), another person standing around the fire accused him: "He is a Galilean." Jesus was from Galilee, and Peter allegedly betrayed himself by his Galilean accent. Terrified, Peter denied Jesus a third time, confirming his denial with oaths and curses (see Matthew 26:74). Immediately the rooster crowed. Jesus, through the courtyard, "turned and looked straight at Peter" (Luke 22:61). The glance touched Peter in the depth of his conscience. He hurried from the place and wept bitterly over his sins. But he did not totally despair, as did Judas. Instead, Peter knew the grace of God in Jesus, and he was forgiven.

Luke 15:1–3, 11–32. The story of the lost son and the forgiving father illustrates a simple truth: God loves and forgives sinners. The "main point" of the story is the gracious welcome extended to the prodigal, or recklessly extravagant, son. The central character is the father: his forgiving love depicts the nature and depth of the heavenly Father's forgiving love.

The heart of the story is, then, the proclamation of the Good News to sinners—to the rebellious, to the broken and despised, to the outcast and unlovable. God does not welcome and receive human beings because of their goodness and achievement. On the contrary, God welcomes and receives *sinners* because He is gracious and forgiving. At all times and for all people, God is the Savior who embraces His repentant children with joy and celebration.

Discussing the Text

1. How did Jesus reverse the ways of the world (Luke 22:27)? See also John 13:35. How did Jesus demonstrate this reversal?

2. We often assume the disciples just sort of walked away from Jesus after He was arrested; however, what does Mark 14:50 seem to indicate? What prophecy does this fulfill (Mark 14:27–31)?

3. Describe in your own words the look and the feelings of both Jesus and Peter, according to Luke 22:61–62.

4. Was Peter any different from Judas in his betrayal? What made the outcome for each different?

Connect

As we consider Peter's denial and repentance, we are reminded of the human condition and God's promises in Christ. The story of humankind is, from one perspective, the story of pride and self-confidence. Adam and Eve were tempted to "be like God" (Genesis 3:5), and in selfish rebellion they turned away from God's Word to pursue their own path—a path that led to death! By nature, all human beings follow their own sinful desires. We are filled with pride and self-confidence, believing that we can stand firm on our own strength or resolve or ability. Yet daily we fall. We are like

Peter, whose boast to follow Jesus "to prison and to death" rang hollow in the face of opposition and potential trouble. Jesus, however, forgives our stubborn pride. In love He restores us, too, just as He restored Peter to salvation and discipleship. In Christ we have full redemption from the curse of the Law, from Satan, and from our own sinful nature.

1. Have you ever felt the way Peter must have felt when Jesus "looked straight at" him after he had betrayed Him? Have you ever received a look such as Jesus must have given Peter? From whom? How did you respond?

2. The rooster crowed three times, reminding Peter that he had failed his Lord (Luke 22:60). What "rooster" helps remind you when you fail the Lord? When you experience guilt for your sins, what do you do?

3. Read Romans 8:35–39. What kinds of temporal adversaries as well as spiritual powers threaten to separate us from God? Record the sure promise from God even though we are not always faithful (Romans 8:37).

Vision

Family Connection

1. Discuss how we sometimes act like Peter. Ask, "How does God respond to us if we deny Him?"

2. Discuss the power of forgiveness. Review the events of the parable of the prodigal son. What were the effects of the forgiveness demonstrated by the father? the lack of forgiveness demonstrated by the older brother?

3. Pray together the Lord's Prayer. Discuss the meaning of the phrase, *Forgive us our trespasses, as we forgive those who trespass against us.*

4. Sing or speak together stanza 1 of "I Am Trusting You, Lord Jesus."

Personal Reflection

1. Write Romans 8:35, 37–39 on a note card and place it in a conspicuous place.

2. Set aside some quiet time and reread the story of the prodigal son, Luke 15:11–32. Afterwards quietly thank God for Your heavenly Father's love.

3. Memorize stanza 1 of "I Am Trusting You, Lord Jesus," printed in the closing worship.

Closing Worship

Sing or read aloud the first stanza of "I Am Trusting You, Lord Jesus."

I am trusting You, Lord Jesus,
Trusting only You;
Trusting You for full salvation,
Free and true.

For Next Week

Read Luke 22:66–23:25 to prepare for next week's session.

Session 5

Pilate Condemns Jesus

(Luke 22:66–23:25)

Focus

Theme: Condemnation for Jesus; Freedom for Us

Law/Gospel Focus

Our sin condemned Jesus! "He Himself bore our sins in His body on the tree, so that we might die to sins and live for righteousness; by His wounds you have been healed" (1 Peter 2:24). Like Barabbas we too are condemned criminals without God's mercy. We have no hope of amnesty except that Jesus trades His innocence for our guilt and with His life, death, and resurrection sets us free from sin, death, and the power of the devil.

Objectives

By the power of the Holy Spirit working through God's Word, we will
1. confess our sin that sent Jesus to the cross;
2. rejoice that Jesus took all our sin with Him to the cross;
3. give thanks that Jesus has set us free from sin, death, and the power of the devil.

Opening Worship

Read responsively the following dialogue-prayer.
Leader: Lord God, the shouts went forth:
Participants: "Crucify Him! Crucify Him!" (Luke 23:21).
Leader: "He committed no sin" (1 Peter 2:22).
Participants: Then why? Why crucify Him?
Leader: "He Himself bore our sins in His body on the tree,

> so that we might die to sins and live for righteousness; by His wounds [we] have been healed" (1 Peter 2:24).
>
> Participants: All praise, honor, and glory to Jesus, the one who "took up our infirmities and carried our sorrows, yet we considered Him stricken by God, smitten by Him, and afflicted. But He was pierced for our transgressions, He was crushed for our iniquities; the punishment that brought us peace was upon Him, and by His wounds we are healed" (Isaiah 53:4–5).
>
> All: Amen!

Introduction

It was before the days of automobiles. People traveled by horse and buggy. One afternoon in a small community in Colorado, a team of horses broke loose and started off down the street. A young boy was directly in the path of the horses. The general manager of the local department store, who was loved by all in the town, dashed toward the boy, pushed him aside, and saved him. The much-loved man, however, was trampled to death by the horses.

Years later when the young boy grew up, he became a town menace. Many times he was caught stealing from the local stores. He was belligerent and at times almost impossible to handle. Often the local townspeople who remembered when he was saved from the runaway horses would say, "And to think he gave his life for him."

1. When Pilate placed before the people Jesus and Barabbas, asking which one they wanted released, they chose Barabbas. Do you suppose that years later, if Barabbas became a repeat offender, the people commented, "And to think He gave His life for him"?

2. How are we like the boy in the story? Do you think it might ever be said of us, "And to think He [Jesus] gave His life up for him/her"?

3. Why was Jesus willing to trade His innocence for our guilt (Romans 11:33)?

Inform

Reading the Text

Read aloud Luke 22:66–23:25.

Jesus stood silently in the great hall. Hours before, He had been arrested in Gethsemane and taken to a hearing before the Sanhedrin, "the council of the elders of the people" (v. 66). The religious leaders had brought many allegations against Him, but the charges were false and contradictory. Even the witnesses could not agree on the "facts." A final question from the high priest determined the verdict: "Are You then the Son of God?" Jesus answered, "You are right in saying I am" (v. 70). The sentence was death. Yet during the feast, with the Roman governor in town, the Sanhedrin lacked the courage to carry out the decision. Jesus, therefore, was shuttled off to Pontius Pilate, the Roman prefect (or governor), for yet another trial.

A Roman official like Pilate had primary jurisdiction over affairs of a province, including, to a certain extent, local policy and procedures. Pilate had authority to confirm the charges against Jesus; he also had authority to dismiss any and all charges and to reduce sentences. Without a doubt, the members of the Sanhedrin felt that Pilate would render the only appropriate judgment: GUILTY! To ensure this, they changed the charges from religious blasphemy to civil insurrection.

Yet Pilate had previously displayed a deep disdain toward Jewish religion and issues. Some nonbiblical writers described his administration of the region as harsh, often insensitive to local customs and attitudes. To bring Jesus for trial before the Roman prefect was to risk an abrupt dismissal of charges or perhaps even more serious repercussions.

Pilate examines Jesus in the Praetorium, the official guest residence of the Roman governor in Jerusalem. Like the high priest, Pilate asks one decisive question: "Are you the King of the Jews?" (The account in John 18:29–38 includes a brief, secondary exchange between Pilate and Jesus; the focus is on the nature of Jesus' kingship—"not of this world.") Jesus' response is a qualified "Yes, it is as you say" (Luke 23:3). He is truly the promised "King of the Jews," but not as Pilate (or the religious leaders or crowds) understand the title. His mission is ultimately not rooted in the political, social, and economic issues of the day. Rather, He is the Savior who has come "to seek and to save what was lost" (Luke 19:10), who will suffer, die, and rise again for the salvation of the world (Luke 24:46–47).

On the basis of the evidence alone, Pilate is convinced of two realities: (1) that Jesus is not guilty of treason against the emperor; and (2) that the chief priests seek Jesus' death out of envy (see Mark 15:10). He therefore attempts to remove himself from the case. First, he sends Jesus to a different judge, King Herod. Second, he offers a Passover amnesty to a "criminal," Jesus or Barabbas. Third, he washes his hands in mock indignation, declaring his innocence and laying blame on the crowd.

Jesus before Herod (Luke 23:6–12). Herod Antipas, a son of Herod the Great, was ruler over Galilee and a portion of the territory east of the Jordan River. (The title *king* was honorific; Herod's actual designation was "tetrarch" [see Luke 3:1].) Though a shrewd politician and generous patron of building projects, Herod Antipas demonstrated little moral integrity in his life and administration. He married the wife of his half-brother Philip; he ordered the execution of John the Baptizer; and he threatened Jesus' life on one occasion (Luke 13:31). When Jesus is brought to him, Herod is "greatly pleased, because for a long time he was wanting to see Him" (Luke 23:8). Herod questions, mocks, and reviles Jesus. But the Lord's silence is judgment against Herod. The Baptizer's stern rebuke rings out amidst the jeers and abuse. Herod shamelessly dresses Jesus in an elegant purple robe—a symbol of royalty—and returns Him to Pilate.

Amnesty at the Passover Feast (Luke 23:18–25). In some ancient cultures, public festivals included an act of clemency, or amnesty, toward condemned persons, especially toward popular local political prisoners. Pilate uses the custom as a political expedient: let the crowd choose, then deny responsibility (see Mark 15:6–11). The other prisoner is Barabbas, a notorious murderer and rebel. He likely belonged to, perhaps even led, a nationalist movement to liberate Israel from Roman rule. Yet Barabbas is the choice; the religious leaders incite the mob to demand the release of the guilty and the condemnation of the guiltless. All these events, though, take place according to "God's set purpose and foreknowledge" (Acts 2:23).

Pilate's declaration of innocence (Luke 23:20–25). Pilate knows Jesus poses no threat to the empire or to public order. His wife, too, recognizes Jesus as a "just man" (Matthew 27:19 KJV), innocent of all charges. Her dream, somewhat mysteriously, reveals the truth; but events unfold by the plan and purpose of God. The crowd presses for Jesus' crucifixion. Pilate faces his dilemma: render justice or satisfy the crowd. The prefect chooses the easy route; he calls for a basin of water, washes his hands, declares his innocence, and sentences Jesus to be flogged, then led to His death (see also Matthew 27:24–26).

Roman scourging was a terrifying punishment. The victim was stripped, bound to a post or thrown on the ground, and beaten by guards. The whip was thick leather strips knotted at the ends, where pieces of bone or lead were often embedded in the thongs. Ancient records indicate that some persons never survived the ordeal. Pilate's soldiers had accompanied the prefect to Jerusalem to keep order during the Passover celebration. The "whole company" consisted of perhaps 600 men. After stripping Jesus of His clothes, they made Him wear a "scarlet robe," probably a soldier's scarlet cloak in imitation of a king's robe. The "crown of thorns" is a crass parody of the royal symbol, as is the staff, a mock "scepter." The common greeting among soldiers was "Hail, Caesar!" The taunt here is "Hail, King of the Jews." Through each stage of the abuse Jesus remains silent, submissive to His Father's will. Struck, spit on, insulted beyond human comprehension, the Son of God goes willingly to the cross and death.

Discussing the Text

1. What charges were brought against Jesus in the following verses:
   a. Luke 22: 67–70

   b. Luke 23:3

   c. Luke 23:5

2. Why do you think the soldiers got so involved in this case (Luke 23:11)? Do you think this was common?

3. Explain the difference between what Jesus meant when He said He was the "king of the Jews" and what Pilate and the religious leaders thought He meant (Luke 23:3–4).

4. After Pilate sees that Jesus is not guilty of treason against Rome, what three things does he do (Luke 23:7; Mark 15:5–11; Matthew 27:24–25)?

Connect

The power of sin is obvious in the jealousy and hatred of the religious leaders and the crowds. God's Law shows the wickedness of their hearts: "You shall not murder" (Exodus 20:13). But human hearts today are no different. We, too, are convicted by our attitudes and actions as "guilty" before the heavenly Judge. We have sinned against all of God's commands, whether we have only stumbled or fallen flat on our faces. Jesus' death takes away *all* sin. He quietly submits to His Father's will. He patiently endures the insults and abuse of sinful human beings. He willingly sacrifices His life on the cross—all for our forgiveness. The Lord accepts His own condemnation at the hands of a Roman governor to save His people from judgment.

Our guilt before God is real. Like Barabbas, we are condemned criminals apart from God's mercy. We have no hope of amnesty, for we have sinned, often deliberately, against the Sovereign of the universe. Barabbas represents every person, for "all have turned away, they have together become worthless" (Romans 3:12). Jesus trades His innocence for our guilt. The sinless Son of God stands before Pilate ready to walk the final distance to Golgotha, where He takes upon Himself the sins of all people. It's the great exchange: Barabbas the murderer goes free while Jesus the Savior gives His life as the ransom. Our life in His death!

1. Share a time when you were falsely accused. How did you react?

2. Pilate thought Jesus was innocent, and yet he gave in to the demands of the crowd! What might you have done under the same circumstances? When have you given in to something even though you knew it was wrong?

3. Compare Luke 23:18–25 with Romans 5:6–11. Who does Barabbas really represent? Compare the account of Barabbas to what Christ has done for us?

Vision

Family Connection

1. Discuss the details of the arrest and trial before Pilate with your family. Ask, "How does it feel when you are unjustly accused of something? How do you respond when such a thing occurs?"

2. Sing the first stanza of "Chief of Sinners Though I Be." Discuss what it means to claim to be the "chief of sinners." How does this claim affect your relationship with others?

3. Thank God together for the magnitude of His love for you that caused Him to send His only Son into this world to suffer and die for your sins.

Personal Reflection

1. Review the story of Barabbas and Jesus (Mark 15:5–11). Think about how much you are like Barabbas; then spend some time in prayer, thanking God for His sacrificial death for you.

2. Review some of your thoughts on the following subjects: abortion; assisted suicide; cohabitation; homosexuality. Is your view about these issues more closely akin to what the world says or what God says?

3. Have you falsely accused someone but not yet apologized, asking his/her forgiveness? If so, ask for his/her forgiveness this week.

Closing Worship

Sing or speak aloud the following stanzas from "Chief of Sinners Though I Be."

> Chief of sinners though I be,
> Jesus shed His blood for me,
> Died that all might live on high,
> Lives that I might never die.
> As the branch is to the vine,
> I am His, and He is mine.
>
> Oh, the height of Jesus' love,
> Higher than the heav'ns above,
> Deeper than the depths of sea,
> Lasting as eternity!
> Love that found me—wondrous thought,
> Found me when I sought Him not.
>
> Chief of sinners though I be,
> Christ is all in all to me;
> All my wants to Him are known,
> All my sorrows are His own.
> He sustains the hidden life
> Safe with Him from earthly strife.

For Next Week

Read Luke 19:28–44; 23:26–56 in preparation for next week's session.

Session 6

Jesus Is Put to Death

(Luke 23:26–56)

Focus

Theme: The Day Time Divided

Law/Gospel Focus

God demands that we keep His Ten Commandments perfectly. The punishment for disobedience is clear: "The wages of sin is death" (Romans 6:23). Though God loves His people and does not desire to punish them, He is also just and righteous and cannot allow sin to go unpunished. Thus, He offered His own Son, Jesus Christ, as our Substitute. He was punished for our sin, for our offenses. He paid our debt by dying in our place. Through His death our broken relationship with God was restored. His death brought reconciliation between God and people.

Objectives

By the power of the Holy Spirit working through God's Word, we will
1. ponder the awesomeness of our Lord's suffering and death;
2. confess that it was because of our sins that Jesus went to the cross;
3. rejoice that Jesus Christ paid the price for our offenses, the price of death itself;
4. thank God for the reconciliation we have with Him because of the life, death, and resurrection of His Son, Jesus Christ.

Opening Worship

Read responsively the following dialogue-prayer.

Leader: Lord God, Your Law is perfect. It demands perfection from us.

Participants: But we fail. We sin. We betray You with our thoughts, words, and actions.

Leader: "What a wretched man I am! Who will rescue me from this body of death?" (Romans 7:24).

Participants: "Thanks be to God—through Jesus Christ our Lord!" (Romans 7:25).

Leader: "There is no difference, for all have sinned and fall short of the glory of God" (Romans 3:22b–23).

Participants: "and are justified freely by His grace through the redemption that came by Christ Jesus" (Romans 3:24).

Leader: "For the wages of sin is death," (Romans 6:23a).

Participants: "but the gift of God is eternal life in Christ Jesus our Lord" (Romans 6:23b).

All: Thanks be to God. Amen.

Introduction

1. How can or do events change the course of history?

2. How did the death of Jesus change lives and, in so doing, change the course of history?

3. The crucifixion of our Lord occurred on what we refer to as Good Friday. Why do we call the day of His death "good"?

Inform

Reading the Text

Read aloud Luke 23:26–56.

Death by crucifixion is among the most brutal forms of punishment in human civilization. Even the ancient pagan world regarded execution by a cross with horror, a type of torture accompanied by a slow, painful death. Rulers depended on the threat of crucifixion to maintain public order; people lived in fear and terror of the "stake and crossbar." The Romans used crucifixion as punishment for treason and other heinous crimes. The comedy writer Plautus says, "Go to the cross!" as an expression of utter condemnation.

In the Old Testament, idolaters and blasphemers were stoned to death, then hanged on a tree or pole—objects of God's wrath and under His curse (Deuteronomy 21:23). When the religious leaders demand crucifixion for Jesus, they not only desire an agonizing death for Him, but that He bear the full shame of condemnation by God (Galatians 3:13).

"They led Him away" (Luke 23:26). Though exhausted from the trials, interrogations, and scourging, Jesus carries His cross to the city gates. His weariness, however, slows the soldiers' progress. A traveler, Simon, is pressed into service. A native of Cyrene, Simon may have been a pilgrim for the Passover feast, in town with his two sons, Alexander and Rufus. Years later, the family may have shared their remarkable story with believers throughout the Mediterranean world.

"A large number of people followed Him" (Luke 23:27). The women among the crowd in particular "mourned and wailed for Him." They are faithful "daughters of Jerusalem," who lament the violence against God's Messiah. Jesus warns that the people will someday lament their own fate, when God's judgment falls on a sinful people for their rebellion and unbelief. (In A.D. 70, some 40 years after the crucifixion, the Romans destroyed Jerusalem and scattered the residents of the Holy City.)

The procession ends at Golgotha. The "Place of the Skull" may refer to the topography (an elevated land mass in the shape of a human skull) or to the routine usage of the site (a place of execution and death). Crucifixion, as with all capital punishment, was done "outside the camp," that is, near but outside the city proper (Leviticus 24:14; Numbers 15:35–38). In this way the wrath of God, as well as the sin of the city/people, was removed (Leviticus 16:27; Hebrews 13:11–14).

Jesus is offered "wine mixed with myrrh" (Mark 15:23), a blend of intoxicants and gum resin to alleviate suffering and extreme pain (Proverbs 31:6). He refuses, however, to drink anything and bears the full brunt of punishment. Jesus is stripped, fastened to the crossbar, and hoisted up to the top of the wooden scaffold. By custom, the soldiers "inherit" the victim's clothing. For amusement and to pass the time, the soldiers gamble—casting lots has both a sacred and secular context—for the garments, belt, and sandals. (St. John mentions the seamless garment, a valuable "prize"—see 19:23–24.) In truth, though, they fulfill the words of the Scriptures: "They divide my garment among them and cast lots for my clothing" (Psalm 22:18).

Jesus is crucified around 9 A.M. By Pilate's direct order, the charges are written in three languages and placed conspicuously on the cross: "King of the Jews." St. John includes the victim's name: "Jesus of Nazareth." The Christian symbol *INRI* comes from the Latin of the full inscription: *Iesus Nazarenus Rex Iudaeorum—"Jesus of Nazareth, King of the Jews."*

The "criminals," whose brief dialogue with Jesus is recorded only by Luke, were predicted by the prophet Isaiah (53:12). The mocking of the crowds and the religious leaders also fulfills the ancient prophecy (Psalm 22:7–8). While on the cross, Jesus speaks seven times. His first words are not a curse on His enemies, but are a prayer for God's forgiveness: "Father, forgive them, for they do not know what they are doing" (Luke 23:34).

Jesus hangs on the cross for six hours before His death. The sky is dark—a miraculous occurrence—from noon (sixth hour) until 3 P.M. (ninth hour). The "Day of the Lord," a time of judgment, included supernatural signs in the heavens (Isaiah 13:10; Amos 8:9). Before the first Passover, too, a plague of darkness covered the land as a token of God's wrath on stubborn Pharaoh and Egypt. The curse of God now, however, falls on the Son of God, who suffers condemnation on behalf of sinful humanity.

Sometime during the ordeal, Jesus calls out the words of Psalm 22:1 in Aramaic, His native tongue (see Mark 15:34). His prayer reveals the depth of His anguish and experience of isolation—separation from His Father. "He's calling Elijah" (Mark 15:35) is a mistaken, though plausible, understanding of His cry, especially with the clamor of the crowd—jeers, weeping, wailing. Some thought that the prophet Elijah would come to aid the distressed people of God (see Malachi 4:5). The drink offered to Jesus was sour wine, or wine vinegar—a cheap, available intoxicant. Jesus, however, is ready for death: His final prayer is "Father, into Your hands I commit My spirit" (Luke 23:46).

"Breathed His last breath" (Luke 23:46). The death is real, not feigned or imagined. The Jerusalem temple had two large veils, one at the entrance to the Holy Place and the other at the entrance to the Holy of Holies (the Most Holy Place). Jesus' death splits the veil at the *inner* sanctuary and thus opens a new and eternal way to the Father (see Mark 15:38; Exodus 26:31–33; Hebrews 9:12).

The earthquake, splitting rocks, opening tombs, and raising of the saints are part of the supernatural signs at the death of God's Son (see Matthew 27:52–53). At this moment, a new community is born. Jesus is the "firstborn" of all who sleep—*die*—and all who rise to eternal life in His name. All believers, from generations past to the present and beyond, share the hope of resurrection and heaven in Christ.

Luke reports that the women who followed Jesus from Galilee watched the crucifixion from "a distance" (Luke 23:49). The women were instrumental in providing for the Master and the Twelve during His ministry. They were also faithful disciples.

Joseph of Arimathea is a devout believer in God's promises (Luke 23:50–51). He is careful to observe the requirements of Deuteronomy 21:22–23. The body of a crucified person was not allowed to hang on a cross overnight. Joseph secures permission to bury Jesus and places the Master in his own new tomb. By coming into contact with a dead body, he becomes "unclean" for the Sabbath.

Discussing the Text

1. Explain Luke 23:28. What happened 40 years later to the city of Jerusalem? to the temple?

2. According to Luke 23:34, what were Jesus' first recorded words on

the cross? Compare these words with the words of Jesus in His prayer taught to the disciples in Luke 11:4. Describe Jesus' forgiveness. See Ephesians 2:8–9 and Romans 5:8.

3. In what ways do the following events in the crucifixion story contradict or prove the Old Testament law of retaliation, "An eye for an eye and a tooth for a tooth" (Exodus 21:24), or Jesus' own words, "A man reaps what he sows" (Galatians 6:7)?
   a. Jesus' death

   b. the first criminal's death (Luke 23:39)

   c. the second criminal's death (Luke 23:40–43)

4. What unusual things occurred with Jesus' death (Luke 23:45–46)? How was the tearing of the curtain significant (Hebrews 10:19–22)?

Connect

The crucifixion is punishment. God threatens to punish all who disregard His Word or violate His Will as revealed in the Ten Commandments. Because of His righteousness, God allows no sin to remain unpunished—period. Crucifixion is the cruelest form of punishment. But Jesus willingly accepts the death sentence—even death on a cross! He offers His life as atonement—full payment— for our offenses. He pays our debt; He shoulders our punishment. He is our Substitute, our Mediator. In His sacrifice, Jesus restores the broken relationship between humankind and God. His death means reconciliation, peace, and life (Romans 5:11; Colossians 1:22).

Jesus' death was real, marked by brutality and indifference on the part of the soldiers. Too often today violence seems to have the last word. Moreover, we have become accustomed to, perhaps apathetic toward, the pain and suffering of people in our nation and around the world. God's Law rebukes our selfishness and lack of concern. Jesus' death, however, demonstrates the extent of His compassion. He is the Good Shepherd who lays down His life for the flock. "He Himself bore our sins in His body on the tree, so that we might die to sins and live for righteousness" (1 Peter 2:24). The Savior of the world suffers for the world so that in Him we might escape the pain and suffering of eternal death. Of course, everyone still dies. But through Christ, God gives us the assurance of His presence at all stages of life, even when we stand at death's portal. We are fully forgiven and blessed forever.

1. The death penalty and the means for carrying it out are controversial. Some say that the electric chair is "cruel and unusual punishment." What do you think? Compare it to death on a cross. Do you think the threat of death on the cross deterred crime in Jerusalem? Do you think the right kind of punishment, even "cruel and unusual punishment," might deter crime in our communities? Explain.

2. Compare and contrast the cross that Simon of Cyrene bore and the cross we are asked to bear for Christ (Mark 8:34). What does it mean to "deny yourself"? Give an example of how that is carried out in your life in regard to your relationship with Christ.

3. Once again, quickly scan the crucifixion story in Luke 23:26–56. Jot down some of the characters in the story and then circle the one character you identify with most. Underline the one character you identify with least. Explain.

4. Recall the first time you heard about the crucifixion of Jesus. Was

any part of the story frightening to you? When did it start to really make sense for you? How do you tell the story to your children, grandchildren, or other children you come into contact with? How do you think it should be told in Sunday school?

5. When people are asked, "How do you hope to get to heaven?" some will answer, "Because Jesus died for my sins!" Is that correct or incorrect? Review 1 Corinthians 15:14–20. Why is it important for us when speaking of heaven to include the truth that we're going to get there because of the life, death, and resurrection of Jesus Christ?

Vision

Family Connection

1. Reread a portion of the crucifixion account each day this week. Discuss the events. Give thanks to God for His love for you and your family.

2. Discuss the different people involved in the crucifixion account. Remember that it is easy for us to look at some of these people and say, "Thank heavens I'm not like him/her." Unfortunately, because of sin all people participated in the crucifixion of Jesus. Discuss with your family what it means that you were the reason for Jesus' death on the cross.

3. Design a family card to send to friends or loved ones. Tell them of the Good News that occurred on Good Friday.

Personal Reflection

1. Write Mark 8:34 on a note card. Place the card in a conspicuous place where you will read it often.

2. Write out a confession of faith using this outline.

I believe Jesus by His life did this for me:

I believe Jesus by His death did this for me:

I believe Jesus by His resurrection did this for me:

3. Review Martin Luther's explanation of the Second Article in his Small Catechism.

Closing Worship

Pray together the following prayer:

Jesus Christ, You became our great High Priest. We thank You. Because You did become our High Priest, we can "approach the throne of grace with confidence." We thank You "that [now] we may receive mercy and find grace to help us in our time of need" (Hebrews 4:16). We thank You. Amen.

For Next Week

Read Luke 24:1–11; Matthew 28:1–10; and 1 Corinthians 15:1–11 in preparation for the next week's session.

Session 7

Jesus Rises from the Dead

(Luke 24:1–11; Matthew 28:1–10;
1 Corinthians 15:1–11)

Focus

Theme: The Central Doctrine of Christianity

Law/Gospel Focus

Because of sin we all must face death; "The wages of sin is death" (Romans 6:23a). Because we sin and because we all must die, the question everyone must answer is this: "What happens to me when I die?" The answer is found in the resurrection of Jesus Christ: "but the gift of God is eternal life in Christ Jesus our Lord" (Romans 6:23b). Jesus promised that on the third day He would rise from the dead. When He did, not only was His promise fulfilled, it showed without a doubt that His payment of death itself was sufficient for our redemption. God accepted the payment. Now the victory of His resurrection is our victory over sin, death, and the power of the devil. We have new life eternally and new life here on earth.

Objectives

By the power of the Holy Spirit working through God's Word, we will
1. rejoice in the Good News of Jesus' resurrection;
2. give thanks that His victory over death is our victory over death;
3. celebrate the new power that is ours as His sons and daughters, the power that raised Christ back to life.

Opening Worship

Read responsively the following dialogue-prayer.

Leader: Lord God, we confess with St. Paul that "if Christ has not been raised, our preaching is useless and so is [our] faith" (1 Corinthians 15:14).
Participants: "But Christ has indeed been raised from the dead" (1 Corinthians 15:20a).
Leader: All praise, honor, and glory to You, risen Lord,
Participants: for resurrecting us to eternal life,
Leader: for resurrecting us to life more abundant (John 10:10),
Participants: for giving to us hope,
Leader: despite our F's and minuses, our can'ts and won'ts,
Participants: there is hope, a fresh breeze, a flash of light, a new tomorrow, a promise,
Leader: hope today and tomorrow, for all the promises of God find their yes in the life, death, and resurrection of Christ Jesus.
Participants: All praise, honor, and glory to You, O Lord, indeed, forever and ever.
All: Amen.

Introduction

We remember May 8, 1945. VE Day was the day victory was won in Europe over Germany. In celebration, people ran through the streets hugging each other and shouting, "We won, we won!" Some never fought; nevertheless, they shouted, "We won!" They claimed the victory.

1. How could people who never fought in the war claim victory?

2. How can we claim *we won* even though Jesus won victory over sin, death, and the power of the devil? What did we do to help win? See Romans 6:1–10.

Inform

Reading the Text

Read aloud Luke 24:1–11; Matthew 28:1–10; and 1 Corinthians 15:1–11.

"The third day He rose again from the dead." In the Apostles' Creed, the church confesses the greatest miracle of all time. The collective witness of the Gospels, as well as the other writings of the New Testament, is this: "THE LORD IS RISEN!" Christian faith is rooted in, and utterly dependent on, the resurrection of Jesus for the life and salvation of the world.

The story of the resurrection cannot, of course, be separated from the death and burial of Jesus. The crucifixion takes place on Friday—Jesus dies around 3 P.M. Joseph of Arimathea, a devout member of the Sanhedrin (the ruling council), requests permission from Pilate to take and bury the body. As a "member of the Council" (Luke 23:50), Joseph has access to the Roman procurator. Pilate is "surprised" that Jesus has died so quickly. Many victims lingered for days, requiring the constant presence of a guard at the site of the crucifixion. (The scourging Jesus endured may have hastened His death.) Joseph's request is urgent; he wishes to provide a prompt but proper burial for Jesus before the beginning of the Sabbath. (The Jewish "day" began at sunset; the Sabbath observance lasted, therefore, from Friday evening to Saturday evening.)

Pilate's consent allows Joseph to remove Jesus' body from the cross, make the necessary arrangements, and place the Lord in the tomb. Joseph is not, however, able to wash and anoint the body. "A stone against the entrance" (see Mark 15:46) lent dignity to the hasty arrangements. It also served as a "guard" against unauthorized entry into the tomb (see Matthew 27:62–66). Some of the women who followed Jesus noted the exact place where He was buried (Luke 23:55) and returned home to prepare spices for the full burial after the Sabbath.

The women (and disciples) rest on Saturday, according to the command of God. Early Sunday morning, Mary Magdalene, Mary the mother of James, Salome, and Joanna (Luke 24:10) start toward the tomb to anoint Jesus' body with a mixture of spices and fragrant oils. Like the disciples, the women have not understood

God's plan to raise the Messiah to life "on the third day." They focus on the work at hand and wonder how they will be able to enter the tomb.

Sometime before the women reach the site, however, the extraordinary sequence of events begins.

1. Jesus rises from the dead. His body, once truly dead, is "made alive" and renewed to new, eternal life. He destroys the power of Satan, sin, and death.

2. The "angel of the Lord" descends from heaven. He rolls back the stone and opens the entrance to the tomb (Matthew 28:2).

3. A "violent earthquake" occurs in the graveyard and throughout Jerusalem (Matthew 28:2). Many saints—God's people—are raised from death to life and testify to the resurrection (Matthew 27:53).

4. The guards at the tomb see the angels, whose appearance is like "lightning." They fall down in terror and remain motionless—most likely in a state of shock. Later, the soldiers recover and return to Jerusalem to make their report to the chief priests and the Council (see Matthew 28:11–15).

5. The women reach the tomb. They enter, but do not see Jesus.

6. The angels appear and announce the resurrection of Jesus to the women. (Luke reports two angels in the tomb; Mark and Matthew mention only the spokesman, perhaps the "archangel.")

7. The angels instruct the women to tell the disciples that Jesus is risen.

Each Gospel account presents important pieces of the whole Easter story—each with distinctive truths about Jesus' appearances to His disciples.

Matthew furnishes vital information on the circumstances of our Lord's resurrection, but in particular he describes the Lord's first appearance to the women. As in Mark, the women flee the tomb "afraid yet filled with joy" (Matthew 28:8). But Matthew immediately reports that Jesus meets the women on their way to tell the disciples (just as the angel commanded; Matthew 28:7). The risen Lord bestows His greeting and comfort. He reiterates the instruction to the disciples, "Go to Galilee." Sometime before His ascension Jesus met the disciples on a Galilean mountain. There He taught and gave the Great Commission (Matthew 28:16–20).

Mark emphasizes the sheer surprise at the Lord's resurrection among the women. The angel's announcement initially provokes only fear and bewilderment. The women flee from the heavenly messenger and the tomb site. On the road home, that is, toward the place where the disciples are gathered, they say "nothing to anyone" (Mark 16:8). Perhaps they stopped to discuss with one another the Lord's teaching about His crucifixion and His promise to rise from the dead. Mark, however, concludes the resurrection account with the women's deep consternation at their unexpected discovery. In this way, Mark draws attention to the proclamation of the Word—the teaching and preaching about the Lord's death and resurrection. The church of Mark's day and today hears and believes the Gospel not on the basis of regular appearances of the risen Lord, but on the basis of His promises. Preachers and teachers carry on the Savior's commission to share the Good News (see Mark 1:14–15).

Luke provides further detail on the appearances to the women and the later appearances to the other disciples. Luke specifically states that after the angel's announcement, the women "remembered His words" (Luke 24:8). Though overwhelmed with emotion ("filled with fear and joy"), they nevertheless believe the Good News. Luke does not report the Lord's appearance to the women on the road; the event is perhaps implied in their faith. Instead, Luke focuses on the apostles' reaction to their report: the apostles "did not believe the women, because their words seemed to them like nonsense" (Luke 24:11). Luke briefly narrates Peter's swift trip to the tomb and his uncertainty over the events of the day. Luke also presents the story of the "Emmaus disciples" (Luke 24:13–35) and the appearances to the disciples (Luke 24:36–49).

John focuses on Mary Magdalene as representative of the women who journeyed to the tomb and later met the risen Lord. The reason, perhaps, is Mary's humble beginning in the community and her utter devotion to Jesus. Luke 8:2 reports that Mary had seven demons cast out from within her; she was eternally grateful to her Lord and Savior. With the other women, Mary reports the Lord's resurrection to Peter and the "beloved disciple" (traditionally, John). The two apostles run to the tomb, but do not find Jesus. Mary, too, returns to the tomb. She is weeping as she peers into the grave, where two angels sit. Her response to the angels' question is evidence of her love and reverence for the Master. She does not, however, recognize Jesus, for He has a glorified body. When the Lord speaks her name, His identity is sure. He is her dear Teacher, Messiah, Savior. Jesus tells Mary to report His resurrection appearance to the apostles, and she quickly returns to share the Good News.

Discussing the Text

1. It was customary for tombs to be tightly closed to keep grave robbers and animals from desecrating the bodies of the deceased. For what additional reason was Jesus' tomb sealed (Matthew 27:62–66)?

2. What physical evidence was there that Jesus did rise from the dead (Luke 24:2–3, 12)? With all this evidence, why was there any doubt that Jesus was alive?

3. Review John's record of how Mary Magdalene was finally convinced of Jesus' resurrection in John 20:10–18.
   a. Why was the question asked by the angels and Jesus appropriate (John 20:13, 15)?

   b. When did Mary finally recognize it was Jesus who was speaking to her (John 20:16)?

c. How might you have responded when you recognized Jesus?

4. How are all three of the these aspects of Jesus' life essential for our salvation?
   a. His perfect life (Galatians 4:4–5)?

   b. His death (1 Corinthians 15:3)?

   c. His resurrection (1 Corinthians 15:17)?

Connect

Death is the consequence of sin (Genesis 2:17; Romans 5:12; 1 Corinthians 15:21–22). The axiom *is* true: "In a perfect world, no one dies." The thought offers little comfort, though, because all people are born sinful and disobey God throughout their lives. Sin is the stark reality, and sin always pays a dreadful wage: death (Romans 6:23). The Good News of Jesus' resurrection revolves around the victory over sin, death, and Satan, as well as the power for new life. The crucified Messiah is now the risen Lord. By the grace of God, Jesus confronts death—He "taste[s] death" (Hebrews 2:9)—in order to redeem His people from their slavery. By the almighty power of God, He then overcomes death to assure His people of forgiveness and eternal life in His name.

The resurrection also reveals Jesus as the compassionate Lord who transforms fear and unbelief into confidence in His Word. Throughout the Old Testament, God's prophets called the people to repentance and faith. But the nation often ignored the Lord's Word despite His miraculous signs: "They did not believe in God or trust in His deliverance" (Psalm 78:22). The message of the angels and the inescapable truth of His appearances is that "He has risen, just as He said" (Matthew 28:6). As He comes to His disciples on Easter Day and in the weeks after His resurrection, Jesus shares His Word of comfort and hope. He is Savior and Lord.

1. Someone once said that many suicides take place because people "have everything to live with but nothing to live for." How does the resurrection change this attitude?

2. What does the resurrection mean for you in each of these areas of your life?
   a. death

   b. sin

   c. Satan

3. Consider Jesus' resurrection. Then answer these two questions.
   a. What happens to me when I die?

   b. What really counts in life?

4. True or False? Why?
   All the promises of God find their yes in the resurrection of Jesus Christ.

Vision

Family Connection

1. Review different resurrection accounts—Matthew, Mark, Luke, and John. Discuss what we learn from each account.

2. Send Easter cards to family and friends. Write a family message that reflects the joy in knowing "He is Risen!"

3. Discuss: What happens when you die? How is this question answered by non-Christians? Christians? What is the reason for the difference?

Personal Reflection

1. Write Ephesians 1:17–20 on a note card and post it somewhere conspicuous.

2. Telephone or write someone who has recently lost a loved one and remind him/her of the resurrection of Jesus Christ.

3. Give thanks to God for providing you the answer to the question, What happens to me when I die?

Closing Worship

Sing or read aloud the following hymn.

> Jesus lives! The vict'ry's won!
> Death no longer can appall me;
> Jesus lives! Death's reign is done!
> From the grave will Christ recall me.
> Brighter scenes will then commence;
> This shall be confidence.

> Jesus lives! To Him the throne
> There above all things is given.
> I shall go where He is gone,
> Live and reign with Him in heaven.
> God is faithful; doubtings, hence!
> This shall be my confidence.

For Next Week

Read John 21 in preparation for next week's session.

Session 8

Jesus Appears at the Sea of Galilee

(John 21)

Focus

Theme: After the Resurrection

Law/Gospel Focus

People's greatest need is reconciliation and forgiveness. Easter offers that assurance—forgiveness from God and for one another! On our own we are unable and unwilling to reconcile. In mercy, God comes to us in the flesh on Christmas to reconcile the world to Himself. On Good Friday He paid the price of death for our sin. On Easter He rises, assuring us that the price has been met. Jesus lives. He lives to bring reconciliation and forgiveness. He lives to bring us hope, reminding us that we are not alone in coping with life or death.

Objectives

By the power of the Holy Spirit working through God's Word, we will

1. give thanks that the resurrection of Jesus Christ has taken care of our greatest needs—forgiveness and reconciliation with God;
2. confess that we often fail to forgive others or seek reconciliation with those who have hurt us;
3. celebrate that He is the "resurrection and the life," now as well as when we close our eyelids in death.

Opening Worship

Read responsively the following dialogue-prayer.

Leader: Lord God, we confess we often forget Your promise of the resurrection;

Participants: "Jesus said … 'I am the resurrection and the life. He who believes in Me will live, even though he dies; and whoever lives and believes in Me will never die' " (John 11:25–26).

Leader: Forgive us, Lord, when we forget, when we act like life and death are something to be afraid of.

Participants: Today, remind us of Your appearance to the disciples fishing on the sea;

Leader: "Throw your net on the right side of the boat and you will [catch fish]," You told them (John 21:6a).

Participants: "When they did, they were unable to haul the net in because of the large number of fish" (John 21:6b).

Leader: Remind us that Your resurrection delivers us from discontent and despair.

All: Grant it in the name of the risen Lord Jesus Christ. Amen.

Introduction

A small community in Texas decided to put on a county-wide Easter pageant. They were especially excited because recently a very important screenwriter and director had retired to their community and was anxious to do some directing and producing. It was decided he would not only direct the pageant but personally select the actors and actresses for the parts. He chose a Catholic nun for Mary Magdalene. He cast the local banker as Pilate. Judas would be played by the school principal. All of the parts were cast except Jesus. He could not seem to find the right person for this important role. Finally, after much searching, he chose a burly oil-field worker. The worker did not have the best reputation; in fact, he was disliked by many of the townspeople.

On the day of the pageant, the burly oil worker played his part well. So did those who were extras, serving as part of the crowd. One little guy who was playing an extra got so emotionally involved that as Jesus was bearing the cross on his back through the streets, he spit in Jesus' face and said, "Crucify Him. Crucify Him."

The burly oil-field worker stopped, wiped the spit off his face, looked at the little man, and said, "I'll be back to take care of you after the resurrection."

1. Contrast the intention of the man playing the part of Jesus with Jesus' action after the resurrection.

2. What would you say to someone who asked, "What does the resurrection mean to you?"

3. What do you think the average person on the street would say if asked, "What does the resurrection mean to you?"

Inform

Reading the Text

Read aloud John 21.

The heavenly messengers who announced the resurrection of Jesus to the women also said, "Go, tell His disciples and Peter, 'He is going ahead of you into Galilee.' There you will see Him, just as He told you" (Mark 16:7). All the disciples had known grief and shame after the Lord's arrest and crucifixion. Peter, in particular, had been plunged into deep grief and shame, for he denied Jesus—three times! When the women returned from the tomb to tell the disciples, Peter, along with the disciples Jesus loved, ran to the place where Jesus was laid to rest (John 20:3; see also Luke 24:12). Later that same day, the risen Lord appeared to Peter (Luke 24:33; 1 Corinthians 15:5). Over the course of 40 days after His resurrection, Jesus was seen alive by the Twelve, the women who followed Him, and many other disciples (see 1 Corinthians 15:5–8). Without a doubt, the angel's message was true: "He has risen!" (Mark 16:6).

John 21 records the third (John 21:14) of Jesus' numerous appearances to His disciples after His resurrection. The date, however, is not specified. The setting is the Sea of Tiberius, also known as the Sea of Galilee and Lake Gennesaret. Seven disciples were present, including Thomas, who was dramatically confronted by the risen Lord and expressed his unshakable conviction, "My Lord and my God!" (John 20:28). The "sons of Zebedee" refers to James and John. Many of these men were professional fishermen. At Peter's suggestion, they went together to fish (John 21:3). Yet their effort—all night—results in no success: "They caught nothing."

Sometime around sunrise, Jesus stood on the shore. Early morning fog or mist may have made it difficult to recognize Him, or the disciples may not have been able to see clearly in the twilight. Perhaps the Lord willed to remain unknown, similar to His resurrection appearance on the road to Emmaus (see Luke 24:16). For whatever reason, "the disciples did not realize that it was Jesus" (John 21:4).

The Lord's greeting, "Haven't you any fish?" was a common question among fishermen. Yet as the Lord who possesses and now fully uses divine power and insight, Jesus knows the truth about these men and their predicament. His greeting, then, discloses a deeper truth about the disciples: they are helpless on their own, individuals who must wait for and rely on God's gracious blessing in their work. Jesus *gives* His blessing. "Throw your net on the right side of the boat" (John 21:6), the Son of God speaks. The disciples in the boat immediately, mysteriously, obey this "stranger's" command. Nature also obeys His voice. To listen in faith to Jesus' Word is to receive life, salvation, and every blessing.

After the disciples netted a "large number of fish" (John 21:6–7), John, the disciple whom Jesus loved, recognized the stranger on shore as the risen Lord. Who else could work such a miracle? The disciples had witnessed many miracles, including another unexpected, miraculous catch of fish (see Luke 5:1–11). In joy and excitement, Simon Peter "jumped into the water" to greet Jesus. Peter had been wearing only underclothing; in modesty and reverence, he "wrapped his outer garment around him." From about a hundred yards offshore, the other disciples, no less eager than Peter, followed in the boat, towing the net filled with fish.

Before eating the breakfast Jesus had prepared, the disciples were able to finish their task, empty the net, and sort through the fish.

"The net was not torn" (John 21:11) is further testimony to the miraculous catch. In His mercy and goodness, Jesus provides for His disciples more than they desire or anticipate.

The meal on the shore was different from an earlier meal in Jerusalem after the Lord's resurrection (see Luke 24:42–49). Jesus apparently did not eat the bread and fish; instead, He simply gave both to the disciples. Like the feeding of the 5,000, also on the shore of the Sea of Tiberius (John 6:1–13), this meal comes from heaven, good gifts from the Savior God. Jesus is the gracious host; He alone provides in time of need. The disciples no longer questioned the identity of the stranger in their midst: "They knew it was the Lord" (John 21:12). Overwhelmed by His resurrection power and His generous provision, they receive His blessings with thankful hearts.

After breakfast, Jesus speaks—one on one—to Peter. The transition from fisherman to shepherd was perhaps difficult for the impulsive, headstrong disciple. While he still continued to "catch men" for the Master (Luke 5:10), Peter will also shepherd God's people—feeding, caring for, and protecting the flock.

The setting was perhaps similar to Peter's experience in the High Priest's courtyard. As Peter stood near the fire, Jesus asked him three questions, each about Peter's relationship to the Lord. "Simon, son of John, do you truly love Me more than these?" means "more than these other disciples love me" or possibly "more than you love to fish" (John 21:15).

In his first response, Peter showed himself less proud and impulsive than in the past (see Luke 22:33). He was content to acknowledge, "Yes, Lord, You know that I love You" (John 21:15). Jesus' second question focused only on Peter. The disciple's second response was identical to the first response, though Peter's voice may have conveyed more passion and confidence. The third response, however, came perhaps after Peter understood the full significance of Jesus' words. Remembering his recent weakness and failure, Peter cried out that the Lord, who knew all things, must certainly know that Peter loved Him and truly repented of his denial in the courtyard.

After each response, Jesus repeated His commission: "Feed My lambs … Take care of My sheep … Feed My sheep" (John 21:15–17). To Peter, as representative of the apostles and the church, Jesus gave His ministry of forgiveness and service as shepherd of the flock (see Acts 20:28; 1 Peter 5:2–4). In this way, Jesus expressed His own tender care for His people. He is the Good Shepherd, the Shepherd and Overseer of souls (1 Peter 2:25, 5:1–4; Hebrews 13:20). Only those who love Jesus dearly are able to serve under Him as shepherds, loving and caring for His sheep and lambs.

Jesus, the true Shepherd, laid down His life for the sheep (John 10:11–18). Peter, too, will follow in Jesus' footsteps, serving the Lord and His church to the end of his life. In his old age, tradition says, Peter "stretched out" his hand and was led to his death by execution—crucifixion upside down. During the years that followed Jesus' commission, though, Peter, aware of his destiny, labored for the Gospel and served God's people courageously and with joy.

Discussing the Text

1. Compare John 21:1–21 with Luke 5:1–11. Why do you think Jesus repeated the miracle for Peter?

2. Some say that Christ's resurrection has much to say about "the pie in the sky" later on, but little about life now. Consider Jesus' appearance to the disciples at the Sea of Tiberius and the question He asks them (John 21:5). What did Jesus communicate about His concern for the "here and now"?

3. What did Jesus instruct the fishermen to do in John 21:6? After they did this, what happened? Why is it so difficult for us to be God-directed instead of self-directed?

4. What is the meaning of John 21:19? What does tradition say about Peter's death?

Connect

Jesus always responds to the needs of His people. Our Redeemer God pours out His blessings on us, rich blessings in all aspects of life. Our most critical need, however, is forgiveness and reconciliation. The prophet Isaiah's words are true: "Your iniquities have separated you from your God; your sins have hidden His face from you" (Isaiah 59:2). On our own, we cannot find God. We cannot bridge the gap between ourselves and the holy, majestic God. In mercy, God comes to us. The heavenly Father gives His Son over to death to reconcile the world to Himself. As the risen Lord Jesus came to the disciples by the Sea of Tiberius, He comes to us today in His Word, in Baptism, and in the Lord's Supper. He brings His forgiveness and life to calm our fear and satisfy our spiritual hunger and thirst.

Jesus gives strength to His disciples. His presence is joy in the midst of emptiness and futility. He enables His people to live with confidence and purpose. "Peter will glorify God." God is glorified by faithful disciples who proclaim His truth and are willing, when necessary, to lay down their lives for the Gospel. "Follow Me!" Jesus' call also extends to us. Knowing that he was commissioned to preach the Gospel, knowing that trials and sufferings were ahead, Peter was faithful in his ministry. He was ready to endure hardship and death for His Lord and Savior. In Christ, we hear and follow the Savior today, too.

1. Read John 11:25. When Jesus says He is "the resurrection and the life," He speaks in the present tense. He desires to deliver us from drudgery, discontent, and despair—even now. Over what are you despairing? Consider the words of John 11:25.

2. The resurrection means many things. Which of the following things about the resurrection do you find most comforting? Explain.

   a. The resurrection means eternal life.

   b. The resurrection means reconciliation with God and others.

   c. The resurrection means He's present here and now.

   d. The resurrection means I'm not coping with life on my own.

   e. The resurrection means forgiveness.

3. If Jesus came and asked you, "How are you doing … with your marriage … your job … your teenage daughter?" how would you answer Him? After you answered Him, what do you think He'd say to you?

4. A priest had a woman in his parish who said she had visions. She even said she spoke to God. The priest doubted her, and so he asked her the next time she talked with God to ask Him what sin he had committed while in the seminary. She said she would.
   A few weeks later the priest asked her, "Well, did you talk to God? Did you ask Him what sin I had committed in the seminary?"
   "Yes, I did," she said.
   "Well, what did He say the sin was?" inquired the priest.
   "He said, 'I don't remember.' "
   Putting aside the question of whether or not the woman really did speak to God, is it correct that Jesus does forget the sins of our past? See Jeremiah 31:33–34. Why is this truth comforting?

Vision

Family Connection

1. Discuss how you would respond to Jesus' question, "Do you love Me?"

2. Review the events of the story. Discuss how God continues to provide for the physical and spiritual needs of your family.

3. Thank Jesus for dying for your sins in spite of the fact that you have repeatedly denied Him by your sin.

Personal Reflection

1. The resurrection of Jesus Christ means reconciliation, not only for us with God, but with others. Who needs to know you have forgiven him/her? Assure him/her of that forgiveness this week.

2. Remind someone who is going through a difficult time in his/her life that Jesus lives. They're not alone in coping with their problems.

3. Remind someone who is plagued over a past sin that he/she is forgiven by God. Not only has God forgiven the sin, He "will remember [it] no more" (Jeremiah 31:34).

Closing Worship

Sing or read aloud the following hymn.
> He's risen, He's risen, Christ Jesus, the Lord;
> Death's prison He opened, incarnate, true Word.
> Break forth, hosts of heaven, in jubilant song
> While earth, sea, and mountain the praises prolong.

For Next Week

Read Acts 9:1–20 in preparation for next week's session.

Session 9

Saul Becomes a Christian

(Acts 9:1–20)

Focus

Theme: God's Love for All Mankind

Law/Gospel Focus

As a Pharisee and strict adherent to the religious beliefs and values of the Jewish religion, Paul persecuted the early Christian church. By his own admission he actually contributed to the murder of many of them. This all changed, however, when the Holy Spirit changed Paul's heart at the time of his conversion. He was called to a new life of faith in Christ Jesus. In this new life Paul proclaimed loud and clear to all people that Jesus is the one and only Redeemer.

Objectives

By the power of the Holy Spirit working through God's Word, we will
1. confess our sinfulness and need for a Savior;
2. compare Paul's life with our own;
3. rejoice that through the power of the Holy Spirit we were brought to repentance and faith;
4. thank God that we not only know but can share the Good News of salvation.

Opening Worship

Read responsively the following dialogue-prayer based on Romans 7:18–25.
Leader: Lord God, like St. Paul we cry, "I have the desire to do what is good, but I cannot carry it out."
Participants: "For what I do is not the good I want to do;"
Leader: "no, the evil I do not want to do—this I keep on doing."

Participants: "What a wretched man I am! Who will rescue me
from this body of death?"
Leader: "Thanks be to God—through Jesus Christ our Lord!"
Participants: You continue to rescue us through Word and
Sacrament.
All: All thanks and praise and glory. Amen.

Introduction

While the pastor is conducting his Sunday morning worship
service, he sees his child misbehaving. As the congregation
begins to sing the next hymn, he walks down the aisle and
motions his son to come to his office. He feels it is a great opportunity for his son to hear a little "Law" so that he can better hear
the "Gospel" in the sermon.

"Son, why are you misbehaving so? You know it displeases your
mother and me," the father says to his son.

The little boy looks up at his dad, and with tears coming to his
eyes he says, "Yes Dad, I know. I don't want to do bad, but I do it
anyhow. I want to do good, but I don't."

The father is flabbergasted. It is as if he is hearing St. Paul himself speak: "For what I do is not the good I want to do; no, the evil
I do not want to do—this I keep on doing" (Romans 7:19). The
father simply looks at his son and says nothing.

He hugs him and says, "I understand, Son. Let's go in and continue to worship our loving Father."

(Reprinted with permission from *Windows into the Lectionary* by Donald Deffner, © 1996,
Resource Publications, Inc., 160 E. Virginia St., No. 290, San Jose, CA 95112, 408-286-8505.)

1. Can you name a specific time this last week when you've felt like
   the little boy?

2. Can you name a specific time this last week when you were especially thankful for God's forgiveness? the forgiveness of another
   Christian?

3. Share a time when a child taught you a special lesson.

Inform

Reading the Text

Read aloud Acts 9:1–20.

"For I am the least of the least of the apostles and do not even deserve to be called an apostle, because I persecuted the church of God. But by the grace of God, I am what I am, and His grace to me was not without effect" (1 Corinthians 15:9–10).

Paul was once a Pharisee, a strict adherent to the religious beliefs and values of his family and teachers. He was dutiful, loyal, and energetic. He was also, by his own admission, a fanatic—a murderer! The story of his change of heart, his conversion and call to ministry, is a tribute to the limitless mercy and goodness of Jesus Christ, the world's only Redeemer.

The Book of Acts includes three separate accounts of Saul's conversion: (1) the actual event (Acts 9:1–31); (2) a summary report before the Jews in Jerusalem (Acts 22:1–12); and (3) a defense speech before the Roman procurator Festus and King Agrippa at Caesarea (Acts 26:1–32). In his own letters, Paul also describes his background, his role in persecuting the first apostles and disciples, and God's dramatic "turn" of Paul in repentance and faith to the Lord Jesus (see Galatians 1:13–24; Philippians 3:2–11; 1 Timothy 1:12–17). Each part, like pieces of a puzzle, offers insights into the "life" and "new life" of the apostle to the Gentiles.

As a Pharisee, Saul was thoroughly trained in the mosaic law. His desire and personal mission were to study and obey the commandments of God and teach others to follow the covenant regulations. When Stephen and early Christians proclaimed that the Law was fulfilled in Jesus and that God accepts people by His grace in Christ, Paul was outraged. The core of his convictions was now threatened; the only recourse was direct confrontation—to destroy both the message and the messengers!

Saul was present at and approved of Stephen's stoning (Acts 8:1). Immediately afterward, he sought permission to arrest and imprison any and all followers of the new faith. His passion for crushing the movement took him far beyond the borders of Israel to the chief city of Syria—Damascus. A letter from the high priest (Acts 9:2) would open doors for his mission and grant access to local synagogues. Since the decrees of the religious leaders were valid throughout the world, Paul was empowered by law to "extradite" Christians to stand trial in Jerusalem. Perhaps Paul was aware of strong resentment and hostility toward disciples in Damascus. Whatever the reason, though, Paul began his attack on the church with the long journey north, accompanied by trusted companions.

The mission to Damascus takes an abrupt detour with the Lord's revelation to Saul. The "light from heaven" may have been a blinding bolt of lightning or a supernatural ray of sunlight; the outcome, however, is the real focus of the story. Saul lies silently on the ground, broken and helpless. "Why do you persecute Me?" both demands an answer and identifies the heavenly voice. The Lord of the universe speaks; He sees the hardships of His people—His body—and therefore acts to oppose the enemies of His church.

The risen Jesus directs Saul "into the city." Saul's companions hear but do not understand the voice (see Acts 22:9). They stand dazed with their leader, their ambitions shattered by the mysterious revelation. Saul, once a powerful predator, is now completely humbled, blind, unable and unwilling to eat and drink.

Ananias is a pious, faithful Jew. He is naturally reluctant to assume a major role in this extraordinary plan. Yet the Lord Jesus directs the mission of His church by His grace and strength. Saul is *His* "chosen instrument" (Acts 9:15). Saul's background, education, personality, even his Roman citizenship are simply "tools" in the Master's hands. The Lord alone calls and saves sinful human beings. The Lord alone equips and sends forth His people to serve in the world. Saul is singled out and commissioned to preach and teach the Good News of forgiveness and salvation to Israel and to the Gentiles. As the Lord was hated, abused, and rejected, so too will Saul suffer for the Savior and His Word.

Ananias faithfully obeys the Lord and brings God's gift of healing, forgiveness, and a new calling to Saul. The persecutor and murderer thus passes from darkness into light! He is baptized and filled with the Holy Spirit. Saul learns that through water and the Word the Lord rescues His people from eternal condemnation. Jesus builds His kingdom through ordinary yet powerful means of His mercy and love. In grace, He brings Saul to faith and into fellowship with the saints.

Discussing the Text

1. As you review the story of Paul's conversion, what one thing strikes you as most incredible? Why?
    a. God's mercy and goodness are limitless.
    b. "If God wants you, He's going to get you no matter what you do!"
    c. "God sure uses some mighty strange people to carry out His work."
    d. "Anyone can change!"
    e. other _____

2. How were the early Christians described according to Acts 9:2? How can Christians be "the Way" to others?

3. How did what happened to Saul physically symbolize that which happens in the heart of every unbeliever when he comes to know the Lord (Acts 9:8–9, 17–18)? See also John 1:4; 8:12.

4. The name *Ananias* means "the Lord is gracious." Why is it so appropriate that a man by this name did what he did in Acts 9:17–19?

5. Compare and contrast St. Paul's conversion to the conversion that takes place in anyone, adult or infant (1 Corinthians 2:14, John 15:16).

Connect

Paul is brutally honest in his writings. Though he thought he was doing God's will in persecuting the church, he soon learned he was wrong—dead wrong! Paul was fighting God. Paul was denying, even trying to destroy, God's plan for the salvation of the world. He was, by his own admission, the worst sinner (1 Timothy 1:15). Yet Paul is no different from any other person: we are all sinners in the sight of God. The Law shows us our sinfulness and offers no hope to save us, to strengthen us, or to soothe our guilty consciences. Like Paul, we see God's mercy revealed in Christ. By His Word, Jesus has converted us—brought us to repentance and faith—and forgiven all our sins. He has called us by His Good News to new life, and now empowers us to serve Him.

Paul recognizes that God's judgment is global. No one, regardless of race or background or achievement, is excluded from the threat of condemnation. Because sin cuts across national boundaries and ethnic divisions, humankind needs full, universal salvation. Jesus is the world's *one* Redeemer. For Paul, no other name will be proclaimed to rulers and peoples throughout the Roman empire. All of Israel's hopes for redemption, all the yearnings of Gentiles for inclusion in God's holy people, are now found in Christ.

(Adapted from *Acts* [Concordia Commentary Series] by Robert H. Smith [St. Louis: CPH © 1970]. All rights reserved.)

1. Compare Ananias's reaction to God to the reaction you would have had under similar circumstances. Is there anyone in your life right now who openly opposes Christianity? If God asked you, as He did Ananias, to talk to that person about Christianity, how would you respond?

2. Read Paul's account of his conversion in Acts 22:1–12. Now write the account of your conversion. Prepare to share it with someone.

3. Read 1 Timothy 1:15. In some liturgical settings we confess that each of us is a "miserable sinner." In what respect is this true about every one of us? Though miserable sinners, what truth do we celebrate according to St. Paul?

4. Ananias obeyed God even though it was extremely difficult for him to do so. Is there an area of your life in which you have difficulty obeying God? In what ways can you receive strength to obey? Talk to God about it in prayer. Then listen to Him speaking to you through His Word.

Vision

Family Connection

1. Ask each family member, "What is your favorite part of the account of Saul's conversion? Why?"

2. Remind your family that God has called each of you to be Jesus' disciples through Holy Baptism. Review the events that occurred at each family member's Baptism.

3. Sing or speak together the stanzas of "Just as I Am."

Personal Reflection

1. Think of one person you dislike a great deal. Then pledge to pray for him/her this week. Pray also tht God would empower you to reach out to that person in love.

2. Thank God for someone in your life who has been an Ananias. Then, if you can, thank the person.

3. Spend some quiet time in prayer asking that God would enable you to be more like Ananias, obedient to God even when the task set before you is difficult.

Closing Worship

Sing or speak aloud the following stanzas of "Just as I Am."

Just as I am, without one plea
But that Thy blood was shed for me
And that Thou bidd'st me come to Thee,
O Lamb of God, I come, I come.

Just as I am and waiting not
To rid my soul of one dark blot,
To Thee, whose blood can cleanse each spot,
O Lamb of God, I come, I come.

Just as I am, though tossed about
With many a conflict, many a doubt,
Fighting and fears within, without,
O Lamb of God, I come, I come.

Just as I am, poor, wretched, blind;
Sight, riches, healing of the mind,
Yea, all I need, in Thee to find,
O Lamb of God, I come, I come.

For Next Week

Read Acts 9:21–31 and 13:1–33 in preparation for next week's session.

Session 10

Paul Begins His Ministry

(Acts 9:21–31; 13:1–33)

Focus

Theme: Chosen Instruments

Law/Gospel Focus

Evidence of sin is everywhere—broken relationships abound. Jesus Christ's life, death, and resurrection brought us back into a relationship with God and with one another. The Gospel of Jesus Christ confronts the wickedness and evil of the world with truth and grace. Just as God worked through St. Paul to share this truth, so He works through us to carry His message of forgiveness and life to people around us. We are His "chosen instruments," commissioned to "make disciples of all nations" (Matthew 28:19).

Objectives

By the power of the Holy Spirit working through God's Word, we will
1. confess our sinfulness and separation from God and others;
2. rejoice in the Good News that through Jesus' death and resurrection God has reconciled us to Him and to others;
3. give thanks that we are privileged to be His "chosen instruments" to carry His message of forgiveness and life to the people around us.

Opening Worship

Read responsively the following:
Leader: Lord God, sin brought separation and isolation;
Participants: but thanks be to You, through the death and resurrection of Your Son Jesus Christ, we were given fellowship and relationship with You, O God, and with one another.

Introduction

Quite often we hear of convicts who "come to know the Lord"
in jail. Some of them make testimonials before the parole board
suggesting that they are different people since their conversion.
1. Why do you think people are often skeptical of such "conversions"?

2. When Paul started to visit Christian churches preaching forgiveness through the blood of Jesus Christ, why were some Christians
skeptical?

3. If a person came to your church with a background similar to
Paul's, how would he be received by the congregation?

Inform

Reading the Text

Read aloud Acts 9:21–31; 13:1–33.

Acts 9:21–31. Paul's hearers were "astonished" (v. 21) at his complete turnabout. Paul had persecuted—and murdered—the Chris-

tians in Jerusalem and had traveled to Damascus on a grim mission. But the man who desired to catch and bind Christians was soon caught and tied with bonds of love by God. The scoffer became a messenger.

People viewed Paul with suspicion or deep hatred, but he "grew more and more powerful" (v. 22) in his faith, his convictions, and his Spirit-given ability to prove from the Scriptures that Jesus is the Messiah, the Savior of God's people. The conspiracy was local; Paul's enemies in Damascus wanted to "kill him" (v. 23). Yet by God's grace and design, he escaped their plot with the help of his fellow Christians.

When Paul "tried to join the disciples" in Jerusalem (v. 26), they feared that he was an infiltrator rather than a genuine "disciple." The abrupt change of course in Paul's career naturally left the leaders of the church suspicious. Paul's great passion for the unity of the church led him to Jerusalem and to those who were in the faith before him. From them he learned not faith itself but how the other apostles confessed and lived their faith. Paul also learned facts about Jesus and the church.

Barnabas introduced Paul to the apostles. Originally from Cyprus, Joseph, called Barnabas, was a man of noble character who faithfully served the Lord in the church at Jerusalem. His later ministry to the believers in Antioch—at the request of the apostles—personifies his nickname: "Son of Encouragement" (Acts 4:36). Barnabas shared the ministry at Antioch with Paul, and the church grew in faith and membership. To the Jerusalem church, however, Barnabas related the story of how Paul had "seen the Lord," and how at Damascus he had "preached fearlessly in the name of Jesus" (Acts 9:27). Through Barnabas's intercession, the Christians of Jerusalem began to regard Paul as a brother. When opposition to Paul arose, the apostles resolved not to lose another missionary and theologian, as they had lost Stephen. They sent Paul to Tarsus, the capital of Cilicia and place of his birth. Paul remained in Tarsus for approximately 14 years.

Acts 13:1–33. Antioch led the way in missions to the Gentiles. The church there commissioned Paul on his three missionary journeys, a term that identifies his work. Certainly Paul did not have a three-part plan to visit foreign lands for mission work among the native populations. Nor did he travel continuously. He remained for long periods in places like Corinth (Acts 18:1–18) and Ephesus (Acts 19:1–41). He had also previously traveled and proclaimed the Gospel in Arabia and Cilicia. It appears that all his journeys were part of a single great movement of the Gospel from the Jews to the Gentiles, from Jerusalem to Rome and to the ends of the earth.

While the church at Antioch was "worshiping the Lord and fasting" (v. 2), the Holy Spirit spoke through one of the prophets. In Acts, prayer and fasting are frequently associated with God's revelation of His plan. It was God's will that the church "set apart" Barnabas and Saul for His work—to share the Gospel throughout the Mediterranean world.

From the moment when Barnabas and Saul were set apart by the Christian community at Antioch, the mission into all the world was carried forward energetically, systematically, and deliberately. The narrative of Paul's journeys itself moved forward step by step toward the goal: Rome.

Barnabas and Saul travel "to Cyprus" (Acts 13:4), perhaps because Barnabas was a native of the island (see Acts 4:36) and a large Jewish colony flourished there. The population was a melting pot of Egyptian, Phoenician, and Greek elements, with a strong Syrian culture.

In "Salamis" (Acts 13:5), the missionaries immediately established a pattern to their work. They first proclaimed the Word of God in the synagogues, turning only later to the Gentiles. To assist them, Barnabas and Saul have "John Mark" (Acts 13:5), who probably served as *catechist,* a teacher who explained God's Word to new believers.

At Paphos, they "met a Jewish sorcerer and false prophet named Bar-Jesus" (Acts 13:6), who served as a court magician or professional wise man. When the proconsul Sergius Paulus summoned Barnabas and Paul, Bar-Jesus (or Elymas; the name means "magician") opposed their message, just as the magicians of the Egyptian court opposed Moses before Pharaoh (Exodus 7:11–12, 22). "Filled with the Holy Spirit" (Acts 13:9), Paul declared that Elymas was not Bar-Jesus, son of Jesus, but a "child of the devil." As Peter spoke God's judgment against Simon the sorcerer (Acts 8:9–25), so Paul was a vehicle of condemnation to Elymas. The magician was struck blind and "groped about" in darkness (Acts 13:11). The proconsul "believed" (Acts 13:12), convinced of the Lord's grace and power at work in human events.

Paul, Barnabas, and their companions traveled from the coastal city of Perga across the Taurus mountains toward Pisidian Antioch, the cradle of ancient Hittite and Phrygian civilizations. Pisidian Antioch had recently received from Emperor Augustus the status of a Roman colony—military veterans had been settled there to maintain peace and order and to spread Roman customs. Paul began his ministry in the synagogue.

The "reading from the Law and the Prophets" (Acts 13:15) and an address by the synagogue leader or a designated representative were regular parts of the worship service. The "synagogue rulers" recognized Paul as a Pharisee, a distinguished guest whose remarks would edify the assembly. The first part of his sermon (Acts 13:17–25) resembles Stephen's speech (Acts 7), with its historical overview of God's way with Israel. The second part (Acts 13:26–37) focuses on the death and resurrection of Jesus and resembles Peter's sermon at Pentecost (Acts 2). It closes with an offer of forgiveness and justification through faith in Christ (Acts 13:38–41).

Discussing the Text

1. How had God prepared Paul for the challenges that lay ahead for him as he plunged into preaching the Gospel to unbelievers (Acts 9:1–9; Acts 22:3)?

2. What may have been people's thoughts as they heard Paul preach in favor of Jesus instead of against Him (Acts 9:21)? When they realized they were wrong about Paul, what did they do (Acts 9:22)? How was Paul protected from harm (Acts 9:25)?

3. How did Barnabas live the true meaning of his name in what he did for St. Paul (Acts 4:36; 9:26–27)?

4. What two things took place among the Christians before they commissioned Paul and Barnabas to go out as foreign missionaries (Acts 13:2–3)? What might we learn from this story about the work we do within the church?

5. What key elements, present in Paul's sermons, are still pres-ent in good sermons today (Acts 13:17–41)?

Connect

Faith in Jesus results in an extraordinary partnership: baptized into Christ, we are now brothers and sisters in the Lord. Paul lived in joyful thanksgiving to God because of the partnership he shared with his fellow believers in different congregations. The Gospel breaks down barriers, prejudices, and hostilities. By nature, human beings are self-centered; we live in a world fractured by sin—*our sin*. Above all, we are separated from God by our selfishness and disobedience. Jesus breaks down the walls: "He Himself is our peace," St. Paul writes (Ephesians 2:14), for in His death and res-urrection He has reconciled us to God. Our Lord brings us into a new relationship with the heavenly Father, "fellowship" with our Savior God. In His grace and strength we live in a Gospel partner-ship with our fellow Christian and in love toward all people.

We cannot escape the reality of sin, evident in the words and actions that ridicule or deny Christ and His gift of salvation. The Gospel confronts wickedness and evil with truth and grace. As the Lord Jesus worked through Paul to accomplish His purpose, so today our Lord works in our lives to fulfill His plan for His chosen people. We, too, are His "chosen instruments" who carry His mes-sage of forgiveness and life to the people around us. Equipped by the Spirit through Word and Sacrament, "armed" with the Gospel, we are Christ's ambassadors to the world.

1. Saul's change surprised many. Would those who knew you as a child be surprised at who you are today? What would surprise them most?

2. Someone once said that when a person gets to heaven he will be surprised by two things: (1) he will be surprised by some of the people who are there; (2) he will be surprised by his own presence. For example, why would it surprise Stephen to see Paul in heaven (Acts 8:1)?

3. Barnabas encouraged Paul. In some respects he served as a mentor. Who has mentored you in your walk with the Lord? To whom have you been a Barnabas?

4. The Holy Spirit spoke to the Christians of Antioch as they worshiped and fasted. We know that the Holy Spirit speaks to us through the means of grace—Word and Sacrament—strengthening our faith and empowering us for service in the church. How might we have greater opportunity for the Holy Spirit to work in our lives?

5. Think about the people God has placed into relationship with you. Is there someone who does not know about Jesus or in fact is practicing a religion that is contrary to Christianity? Do you think you have a God-given responsibility to that person? to God? How could the class help serve as a Barnabas to you as you set out to talk to this person? How can you serve as a Barnabas to someone else in your class who has someone he/she would like to talk to about Jesus?

Vision

Family Connection

1. Discuss the name *Barnabas.* Identify ways in which members of your family can be a Barnabas to each other.

2. Consider ways in which your family can share Jesus' love with family members or neighbors who do not know Jesus as their Savior.

3. Pray together, thanking God for calling you to faith through the Gospel and continuing to strengthen you in your faith through Word and Sacrament. Ask that the Holy Spirit empower you to witness boldly your faith in Christ Jesus.

Personal Reflection

1. If the person(s) who has served as a Barnabas in your life is still alive, write him/her a letter, thanking him/her.

2. Serve as a Barnabas by writing someone a letter who needs some extra encouragement at this time.

3. Listen carefully to the structure and content of the sermon this week. Identify the Law and the Gospel. Pray for the pastor as he preaches the sermon, asking that God give him words that will powerfully bless you and the other listeners.

Closing Worship

Pray the following prayer:
> Lord God, You are the Way, the Truth, and the Life.
> Help us to show others:
> > the Way You have shown us,
> > the Truth You have given us,
> > the new Life You have placed into us,
> For Your love's sake. Amen.

For Next Week

Read Acts 13:44–52; 16:1–5 and 2 Timothy 1:5–7; 3:14–16 to prepare for next week's session.

Session 11

Paul Preaches to Jews and Gentiles

(Acts 13:44–52; 16:1–5; 2 Timothy 1:5–7; 3:14–16)

Focus

Theme: For All the People of the World

Law/Gospel Focus

Sin is evident in all mankind: "All have sinned and fall short of the glory of God" (Romans 3:23). As today, some early Christians believed that the Good News of salvation was reserved for them and them alone. St. Paul made it clear that just as "all have sinned," so all "are justified freely by His grace through the redemption that came by Christ Jesus" (Romans 3:24). No person, ethnic group, or culture is exempt from the verdict of the Law, but at the same time neither is anyone who believes in the saving work of Jesus Christ exempt from forgiveness and eternal salvation. The Holy Spirit empowers the Christian church to bring that Good News to everyone.

Objectives

By the power of the Holy Spirit working through God's Word, we will
1. acknowledge that no person, ethnic group, or culture is exempt from the verdict of the Law;
2. give thanks that no person, ethnic group, or culture is exempt from forgiveness and eternal salvation through faith in Jesus Christ;
3. go forth in joy, thankful for the privilege of being able to share this life-saving Gospel with all people.

Introduction

There is a story told of when Jesus ascended back to heaven after His resurrection.

As He stands before His Father's throne, His Father asks Him, "Son, are You alone?"

Jesus reaches out His hand and shows Him the world, saying, "No, My Father, I brought My brother along!"

1. If such a scene should take place when you die, and you are asked, "Son (Daughter), are you alone?" what would you say?

2. Someone has said the only things you can take with you to heaven are your children and your grandchildren. How is that really true?

3. Who do you pray will be there alongside you when you reach heaven someday? What are you doing to assure this happens?

Inform

Reading the Text

Read aloud Acts 13:44–52; 16:1–5; 2 Timothy 1:5–7; 3:14–16.

Acts 13:44–52. Paul's preaching left a powerful impression on his audiences. At Pisidian Antioch, "almost the whole city" turned out to hear the Word of God, the Good News of salvation and life in Jesus.

The attitude of the more conservative Jews hardened when they saw great numbers of Gentiles taking an interest in the Gospel. "They were filled with jealousy" (see also Acts 5:17), afraid that the line between clean and unclean, between Jew and Gentile, would be erased by Paul's proclamation of Jesus as the Son of God and promised Messiah. Some "talked abusively" against Paul and perhaps also against Jesus (see Acts 26:11; 1 Corinthians 12:3).

In the face of opposition, Paul and Barnabas announced, "we now turn to the Gentiles" (Acts 13:46). Their mission was to preach first to the Jewish people, then also to the Gentiles (see Acts 3:26; Romans 1:16; 2:9–10). Israel's rejection of the Gospel was a great tragedy, the result of hearts hardened to God's plan and purpose (Acts 13:40–41). The progress of God's salvation among the Gentiles was, of course, good and joyous. But, sadly and tragically, it spelled the alienation of the church from the synagogue.

God's love for Gentiles is expressed in the Old Testament and specified in Jesus' commission (see Matthew 28:16–20; Acts 1:8). Jesus Himself is called "a light for revelation to the Gentiles and for glory to

Your people Israel" (Luke 2:32; Isaiah 49:6). Paul and his co-workers brought light and were light for the Gentiles. The One who said, "I am the light of the world" (John 8:12; 9:5) also said, "You are the light of the world" (Matthew 5:14). The salvation of God is destined for the "ends of the earth" (Acts 13:47).

The Gentiles, among the predestined and elect of God (Romans 8:28–30), rejoiced in the dawn of the new age. They came to faith and their names were written in the book of life. Immediately these Gentile Christians became missionaries, and "the Word of the Lord spread through the whole region" (Acts 13:49).

Zeal for the Law changed to jealousy and rage, and some of the Jewish leaders used prominent citizens of Pisidian Antioch to raise powerful opposition against Paul and Barnabas, who were expelled and banished from the city. Paul and Barnabas, in turn, "shook the dust from their feet in protest" (see Luke 9:5; 10:10–11), a symbol of the complete rupture of relations and fellowship, abandoning the city to the just judgment of God.

Paul and Barnabas probably walked to Iconium. Although their stay at Antioch may have been only for a week, it produced "disciples," followers of Jesus who "were filled with joy and with the Holy Spirit" (Acts 13:52).

Acts 16:1–5. An ancient road, improved by the Romans, led from Syria across the mountains and around the gulf to Tarsus. Travelers then turned abruptly northward through the narrow gorges of the Tarsus Mountains known as the Cilician Gates. The army of Alexander the Great had marched through this passageway on the way to Persia. Paul walked westward to Derbe, connected to Lystra and Iconium by another Roman highway. Lystra was the home of a "disciple named Timothy" (v. 1). Whether he had been converted by Paul is not mentioned by Luke. Timothy was the son of a pagan father, but his mother, Eunice, was a Jewish Christian, as was his grandmother, Lois.

Paul objected to the *necessity* of circumcision for salvation (see Acts 15:1–2), but he himself performed the rite on Timothy for tactical reasons. If Timothy were circumcised, he would have ready access to synagogues as a co-worker with Paul.

Paul was faithful to the apostolic council (Acts 15), not as a subordinate to the Jerusalem apostles, but as a partner who rejoiced in the unity of the church. He "delivered the decisions," that is, the content of the letter drafted by the council (see Acts 15:23–29). Paul did not establish these congregations, but revisited and strengthened the believers "in the faith" (Acts 16:5).

Discussing the Text

1. Why did the Jews often oppose Paul and the early apostles (Acts 5:17; 13:45)? Cite some modern-day examples of jealousy among churches.

2. Review the disciples' words in Acts 13:46–47. Were the words Law or Gospel? Though it must have been hard, Paul preached the truth. Why did the Jews have difficulty accepting the words of St. Paul?

3. What does the word *appointed* mean (Acts 13:48)? Have you been appointed to receive eternal life? Is it the same as *predestined?* See also Romans 8:28–30 and Ephesians 1:4.

4. What do we know about Timothy's religious background (Acts 16:1; 2 Timothy 1:5; 3:15)?

5. What truth had Timothy learned from Scripture (2 Timothy 3:14–17)? According to these verses, how does Scripture offer practical instruction?

Connect

The apostle's singular purpose in life is to witness to the grace of God in Jesus Christ. He desires to reach His fellow Jews first, but he recognizes and obeys the Lord's call to preach the Good News to all different peoples—"the Gentiles." For Paul, the simple fact revealed in Scripture and evidenced in human behavior is "all have sinned and fall short of the glory of God" (Romans 3:23). No person, ethnic group, or culture is exempt from the verdict of the Law: "the wages of sin is death" (Romans 6:23). But the Gospel, the gift of God's grace in Jesus Christ, is life (Romans 3:24; 6:23). In the Savior's death, the whole world has been redeemed, that is, declared "not guilty" before the righteous Judge. The task of all early Christian missionaries was to bring that Good News to everyone so that men, women, and children may know and receive God's salvation by faith. By God's grace, it is our task, too!

1. The apostles spoke the truth even though at times it meant rejection (Acts 13:45–47). There is a perception among some Christians that because God calls us to love one another we must never admonish anyone. What is wrong with such thinking? Is there someone you have failed to admonish even though he/she is doing something contrary to what God says (e.g., a son or daughter cohabitating with his/her boy/girl friend)? Why is tolerance of evil itself evil?

2. True or False? Why?
   a. God predestined some because He foreknew who would believe and who would not.

   b. The fact that God chose us before eternity should bring us great comfort and consolation.

    c. Predestination is another verification that salvation comes only by God's grace without any merit or worthiness on our part.

    d. God is so certain of those who are predestined that He already sees them with glorified bodies in heaven.

3. Why is it so important for us to believe that all of Scripture is inspired, or "God-breathed," as St. Paul reminds Timothy (2 Timothy 3:16)? As a parent, how does the inspiration of Scripture help you? or as a friend speaking to another friend about his/her wrong-doing?

4. Are there people of different nationalities or ethnic groups within the circumference of your church who need to hear the Word of God? What about where you work? As important as it is to model your Christianity in the way you live your life, why are words so important? What are some ways you might share God's plan of salvation with others?

Vision

Family Connection

    1. Read together 2 Timothy 3:15–16. Then make a commitment to spend at least a few moments together each night reading a small portion of the Bible.

    2. Bibles are often kept on a bookshelf or in a drawer. Discuss where you might place your family Bible so that you will see it and use it often and where people who visit your home will see it.

    3. Have every member of the family pick one of his/her favorite verses. Read it aloud from a variety of versions. Invite the person

who selected the verse to share why the verse is especially meaningful.

Personal Reflection

1. Memorize 2 Timothy 3:15–16.

2. Ask the pastor to give you some materials on predestination or go to your church library and research the topic. Make sure you carefully study the scriptural passages and let them speak to you even if you can't logically understand them.

3. Ask yourself, "Am I tolerating some evil right now for the sake of peace?" If so, resolve this week to speak the truth of God's Word in love (Ephesians 4:15).

Closing Worship

Partner up with someone in class and speak the following blessing to one another:

"May the Lord Jesus Christ fill you with spiritual joy. May His Spirit make you strong and tranquil in speaking God's truths to one another. And may the blessing of the Lord come upon you and the ones to whom you speak. Amen."

For Next Week

Read Acts 14:8–23 and 16:6–15 to prepare for next week's session.

Session 12

Paul Proclaims the Good News in Lystra, Derbe, Macedonia, and Philippi

(Acts 14:8–23; 16:6–15)

Focus

Theme: Being Politically Incorrect for the Sake of the Gospel

Law/Gospel Focus

Like today, the early Christian church encountered evidence of sin everywhere: idolatry, sexual immorality, discord and dishonesty, every type of selfish ambition, and evil. Paul's preaching ran counter to what the people of his day and age believed in and worshiped: pagan temples, altars, sacrifices, statues of false, idolatrous gods. His preaching was "politically incorrect" and yet he preached boldly because he knew it was the Word of God, that which is true and powerful. And God used the Word in powerful ways to change many people and begin new mission stations, just as He uses the Word today to change lives and spread His message of love throughout all nations.

Objectives

By the power of the Holy Spirit working through God's Word, we will
1. acknowledge that God has a wonderful plan for His chosen people, just as He had a plan for Paul;
2. identify some ways we might better share the message of salvation with all people both near and far;
3. give thanks that despite obstacles we may face in our

proclamation of the Gospel, the Holy Spirit empowers us through Word and Sacrament to strengthen our faith so that we may witness boldly.

Opening Worship

Read responsively the dialogue-prayer based on Matthew 28:19–20.

Leader: Lord God, for the privilege of proclaiming Your words of life and death to others, we thank You.

Participants: "Therefore go and make disciples of all nations, baptizing them in the name of the Father and of the Son and of the Holy Spirit."

Leader: We want to, Lord, but we're afraid.

Participants: Forgive us and make us bolder, even now as we study Your Word.

Leader: Loosen our tongues and open our hearts to the cries of those who do not know You,

Participants: "teaching them to obey everything [You] have commanded [us]."

Leader: We want to, Lord, but we're afraid.

Participants: Forgive us and make us bolder, even now as we study Your Word.

Leader: Remind us, assure us,

Participants: "...surely [You are] with [us] always, to the very end of the age."

All: We believe it. We will go forward in the name of Jesus Christ. Amen.

Introduction

Many people spend a great deal of energy making sure that what they say and do is "politically correct."

1. What are some examples of politically correct words and/or actions?

2. How might sharing the truth of God's Word at times be considered politically incorrect?

3. Why is it dangerous to place concern for political correctness over sharing God's Word in its truth and purity?

Inform

Reading the Text

Read aloud Acts 14:8–18; 16:6–15.

Acts 14:8–18. Lystra and Derbe were cities of Lycaonia (see also Acts 16:1–2). Little is known of Paul's ministry in Lystra except for a single healing, which was similar to Peter's healing of the lame man in the temple (3:10). Both paralleled Jesus' healing of the paralyzed man (Luke 5:18–26). The ministry of Jesus continued first in Jerusalem among the Jews through the hand of Peter and later in all the world among the Gentiles through the hand of Paul.

The lame man "sat," "crippled in his feet"—he was "lame from birth" and "had never walked" (v. 8). But his ears were good, and "he listened to Paul," who perceived that the man had faith (see Acts 3:16; 4:9; Luke 5:20; 7:50; 8:48; 17:19; 18:22). Prompted by the Holy Spirit, Paul spoke the creative word of God's grace in Christ and the man was made whole and "began to walk" (v. 10).

The Lycaonians thought the gods had come to visit them in the likeness of human beings. (According to local mythology, all gods and goddesses came to earth secretly in human guise and lived, loved, and played in various towns and villages.) Since Barnabas was likely the older of the pair and Paul the more eloquent, the Lycaonians identified them as Zeus, the chief of the gods, and Hermes, his son and messenger of the gods.

The "priest of Zeus" (v. 13) may have witnessed the healing, since the lame man probably sat in front of the temple near the gate of the city (see Acts 3:2). The apostles did not understand at first what was happening, because the people spoke their native Lycaonian. But when Paul and Barnabas saw the "bulls and wreaths," customary in a ritual sacrifice, they grasped at once that *they* were being offered divine honors. Both were horrified at the crass display of idolatry, a blatant act of confusing mere creatures with the one, true Creator. As a sign of distress or shock, Paul and Barnabas "tore their clothes" (Acts 14:14).

This may be Paul's first sermon to a pagan audience. It resembles, in many respects, his later, more famous speech in Athens on Mars Hill (Acts 17:16–31). Rather than rehearse God's saving acts in the Old Testament as background to the Gospel, Paul witnesses to God's work in creation. Rather than testimony to God as the Lord of history, Paul's emphasis is on God as the Lord of the universe and the Giver of life. Instead of immediately proclaiming Jesus as the Messiah—an unknown concept to pagan populations—Paul begins with the truth of one God, who alone blesses humankind with His gifts from heaven.

Paul's message was a direct assault on any and all idolatry: "We too are only men, human like you" (Acts 14:15). He was only a messenger of "good news," revealed by the God who calls every person to turn from "these worthless things": pagan temples, altars, sacrifices, statues of false, idolatrous worship.

Paul's call to "turn" echoes the great Old Testament prophets' word, "repent!" Instead of an idol of wood or stone, faith in Christ offered pagans fellowship with the true and "living God, Creator and Savior of the universe." God had been patient in times past (see also Acts 17:23, 30; Romans 2:4; 2 Peter 3:9, 15). In mercy He gives all people—believers and nonbelievers alike—"rain from heaven and crops in their seasons," as well as "joy" in life (Acts 14:17). God gives every good and perfect gift, and every good thing witnesses to His patience toward the world. Paul, like Elijah on Mount Carmel (1 Kings 18:20–40), was attempting to win the devotion of the people for the one God who alone gives life, blessings, and salvation.

Acts 16:6–15. Paul and his party had been traveling westward from Cilicia. They had evidently planned to follow the Lycus River and visit

Colossae, Hierapolis, and Laodicea.

The missionaries tried several successive routes. But the "Spirit of Jesus" (v. 7) blocked each path until only the road to Troas still lay open and untried. It is not known through what means they experienced the negative guidance of the Spirit. It may have come through a dream, vision, or prophetic utterance (see, for example, Acts 9:10; 10:3; 13:2; 18:9). Illness or physical inhibition could also have conveyed the Spirit's message. The expression "Spirit of Jesus" means the Holy Spirit given to believers. The mission is not Paul's. It is the Lord Jesus' mission, which empowers, guides, and gives success to the church's ministry. The "man of Macedonia" serves as God's messenger, calling Paul and his companions (including Luke) to Europe.

In Europe, Paul continued to seek out the local Jewish community at every opportunity. "On the Sabbath" (Acts 16:13) the missionaries went outside the city in search of a "place of prayer," the equivalent of a synagogue. Water was necessary for the washings connected with formal prayer, so synagogues were frequently located near rivers or running water. Since they found "women" gathered without men, it is likely that the "place of prayer" was an informal meeting site and not an established synagogue.

The first convert outside Palestine and Asia Minor was a woman: Lydia. Her home was the "city of Thyatira" (Acts 16:14) in the country also called Lydia, and she was apparently a prosperous merchant, selling the famed Thyatiran dyed goods. In the ancient world, purple was the color of royalty. Lydia may have provided fine cloth and other quality goods to various imperial families in the Mediterranean basin and beyond. She had been a "worshiper of God," that is, a Gentile who accepted the teachings of Judaism. Now, however, by the grace of God and the work of the Holy Spirit, she believed the Good News of forgiveness and salvation in Jesus. Without delay, Lydia "and members of her household" were baptized; it is likely that her children, servants, and other dependents were brought to faith through the "washing of rebirth and renewal by the Holy Spirit" through water and the Word (Titus 3:5).

As Cornelius had done previously (Acts 10:48), Lydia opened the doors of her house to the Christian missionaries. She even prevailed on them to make her residence a kind of headquarters during their stay in Philippi (see Acts 16:40). The Philippian Christians received Paul's love and concern, and they showed Paul support and kindness throughout his ministry and during his imprisonment (see Philippians 1:3–18; 4:10–19).

Discussing the Text

1. What is the secret to all healing as indicated in the account of the crippled man (Acts 14:9)? Note also Luke 5:20; 7:50; 8:48; 17:19.

2. Describe what the scene must have been like when Paul and Barnabas were thought to be gods from another world (Acts 14:11–13). How could the apostles have taken advantage of the situation and benefited greatly from their fame? Can you think of some recent situations in which people were attributed godlike fame and took advantage of the situation for their own good?

3. Examine one of the first sermons preached to a pagan audience by Paul and Barnabas (Acts 14:14–17). Describe Paul's approach. Why is this approach so important?

4. Who was the first convert outside Palestine and Asia Minor (Acts 16:14–15)? If Lydia was a Gentile, what God did she worship? Who opened Lydia's heart? Who opens our hearts? Through what means does He open our hearts?

Connect

Even as Paul faces natural disasters and extraordinary perils, God directs him to preach the Good News of Christ to the nations. Besides the accounts in Acts, Paul shares a list of his personal hardships in ministry in 2 Corinthians 11:23–29. The early Christians shared the message of salvation with joy to all people, a message filled with urgency. Human wickedness was rampant in their day: idolatry, sexual immorality, discord and dishonesty, every type of selfish ambition and evil. God's word of condemnation for human sin—the Law—was not a distant, idle threat, but a present reality! With great boldness, the apostle Paul proclaimed the truth of a righteous, almighty God who will judge unrepentant sinners. With equal boldness, though, he proclaimed the Good News of forgiveness and new life in Christ.

By God's grace a new relationship has been established: we are His redeemed children, ransomed by the death of Jesus on the cross. Called by the Spirit, gathered around the Gospel, we, like the believers of Paul's day, move forward in faith and ministry.

1. Can you think of any challenges you face similar to the ones Paul and Barnabas faced in Acts 14:14–20? Are there things you advocate and uphold as a Christian that make people consider you "politically incorrect"? Where can you receive courage to face opposition?

2. Consider someone you know who is an unbeliever. Review Paul's words to the people of Lystra (Acts 14:15–17). Divinely inspired, the words spoke to the immediate needs of the people. As you think about the person who is an unbeliever, what words might you speak that would help him/her clear up some misunderstanding he/she might have?

3. "The Lord opened [Lydia's] heart to respond to Paul's message" (Acts 16:14). When did you "respond" to the Good News of salvation? Whom did God give you to open your heart to the message of God's love and forgiveness through faith in Christ Jesus? Name some people God has used in your life to help you grow in your faith.

4. Even though Paul had his own ideas about where he wanted to go to spread the Good News of salvation, God had other ideas. In the spreading of the Gospel or whatever we do, we must remember God is the Maker of our tomorrows. How does James 4:13–15 speak to your plans?

Vision

Family Connection

1. Allow each person in your family time to share their faith journey. Urge each to share how, who, when, and where.

2. Discuss how God might use each member of your family to "open hearts" to Jesus' love.

3. Sing or speak together "Fight the Good Fight," printed in "Closing Worship."

4. Share opposition you might face to sharing the love of Jesus with others at the office, in school, on the playground, etc. Pray that the Holy Spirit might empower you to share God's Good News of Jesus Christ even as you face opposition.

Personal Reflection

1. Think of someone God has placed in your life who needs to hear about Jesus. Then, this week, make every effort to talk to him/her about Jesus.

2. Read a different psalm each day this week and ask God to "open your heart" to a correct understanding of the words and what they mean for you.

3. Write Jeremiah 29:11 on a 3 × 5 card and post it in a place where you will read it often.

Closing Worship

Sing or read aloud the following stanzas of "Fight the Good Fight."

Fight the good fight with all your might;
Christ is your strength, and Christ your right.
Lay hold on life, and it shall be
Your joy and crown eternally.

Run the straight race through God's good grace;
Lift up your eyes, and seek His face.
Life with its way before us lies;
Christ is the path, and Christ the prize.

Cast care aside, lean on your guide;
His boundless mercy will provide.
Trust, and enduring faith shall prove
Christ is your life and Christ your love.

For This Week

Read Acts 16:16–40 to prepare for next week's session.

Session 13

Paul Proclaims the Good News to a Jailer

(Acts 16:16–40)

— Focus —

Theme: The "Jailhouse Rock"

Law/Gospel Focus

As we share the Word of God with others, we meet opposition and hatred; nevertheless, we share it knowing that the very Gospel we share is the "power of God for the salvation of everyone who believes: first for the Jew, then for the Gentile" (Romans 1:16).

Objectives

By the power of the Holy Spirit working through God's Word, we will

1. acknowledge that since all people are sinful from birth and separated from God by nature, they will be hostile toward the preaching and teaching of the Law and the Gospel;
2. thank God that through the Holy Spirit unbelief and hostility are turned into belief and love for God;
3. become even more zealous in sharing the Good News of salvation whenever the opportunity arises.

Opening Worship

Pray responsively the following prayer.

Leader: Lord God, is there any better news than the words spoken to the jailer of Philippi?

Participants: "Believe in the Lord Jesus, and you will be saved—you and your household."

Leader: The jailer was "filled with joy because he had come to believe in God."

Introduction

1. What's one of the toughest situations you've ever experienced? What do you recall doing during this time? Did you pray? If so, describe the prayer.

2. Which television program best describes how you pray when you're under pressure? Why?
   a. "Let's Make a Deal"
   b. "Father Knows Best"
   c. "Scared Stiff"
   d. "The World's Funniest Videos"
   e. other _____

3. Do you ever sing while under pressure? If so, what songs do you recall singing?

Inform

Reading the Text

Read aloud Acts 16:16–40.

Paul continued to meet Jews and God-fearers at the river. On the way he was confronted "by a slave girl who had a spirit by which she predicted the future" (Acts 16:16). Literally, she had a "pythonic spirit," that is, she was possessed by a demon posing as the god Apollo,

108

whose symbol was the snake and whose business was telling the future. The owners of the girl charged a fee for her prophecies and revelations (Acts 16:19).

A demon-possessed man had once correctly named Jesus "the Holy One of God" (Luke 4:34). Here, a demon-possessed girl cried out that Paul and his companions were "servants of the Most High God" (Acts 16:17; see also Daniel 3:26). She also recognized that they proclaimed "the way to be saved." No pagan god or goddess can offer the way of rescue; only the true God, revealed in the Scriptures and in Christ, brings hope and assurance of salvation.

Loud shouts by demon-possessed people disclosed the real identity of Jesus in the Gospels, and here, too, the girl's shouts correctly identified Paul and his mission. Paul drove out the evil spirit "in the name of Jesus Christ." The spirits are obedient to Jesus, the Lord who alone brings redemption.

The deed earned the hostility of the girl's owners, who stirred up public resentment and official action against Paul and Silas. The owners banked on anti-Jewish sentiment to make good their revenge. Paul and Silas were dragged "into the marketplace to face the authorities" (Acts 16:19). The charges were promoting a strange and illegal religion among Roman citizens.

If the judicial proceedings began fairly, they immediately deteriorated as the crowd, in a fit of racial and religious prejudice, demanded swift punishment. Without further inquiry, the magistrates had the apostles stripped and "severely flogged" (Acts 16:22). Paul and Silas were then handed over to the warden of the prison and safely locked in "the inner cell," a dungeon, with their feet secured in stocks.

Paul and Silas, extremely uncomfortable because of the beating and the stocks, did not sleep or groan or complain in prison. Rather, they were "praying and singing hymns to God" (Acts 16:25). Their fellow prisoners were listening, and God also heard the apostles. His answer was a "violent earthquake" (Acts 16:26), which shook the prison at midnight. The doors were opened; the chains were loosened. The jailer was terrified, fearing that the prisoners had escaped and he would be held accountable. The only honorable solution was suicide.

The voice of Paul reassured the jailer and kept him from self-destruction. The jailer's fear of death became true fear of God, and he threw himself in front of Paul and Silas: "Sirs, what must I do to be saved?" (Acts 16:30).

Paul answered that faith in "the Lord Jesus" is the way to salvation. The jailer and his family believed and responded by washing and refreshing Paul and Silas. The apostle then baptized the entire household, and together they rejoiced in God's mercy.

The magistrates waited until daybreak before they dismissed Paul and Silas. The message of release went from the magistrates to the officers to the jailer to Paul. But the apostle refused to be dismissed so easily and impersonally; for the first time he revealed that he and Silas were "Roman citizens" (Acts 16:37). The magistrates were shaken, because they knew they had acted badly on two counts: imprisonment without trial and beating a Roman citizen.

Paul and Silas could have demanded severe justice, but they settled for a formal apology on the part of the magistrates, who then politely requested that the missionaries "leave the city" (Acts 16:39). They could not take responsibility for the safety of two unpopular men who were disturbing the peace. Paul and Silas, however, were not to be hurried. First, they "went to Lydia's house" (Acts 16:40) and spent time with the new Christian community, encouraging the believers before leaving Philippi.

Discussing the Text

1. Describe today's counterpart to the woman spoken of in Acts 16:16–19. Why were Paul and Silas treated so harshly for healing a possessed woman? What are some similar incidents today where money is made from sinful behavior? Why does opposition by Christians anger those who profit because of it?

2. Describe the people's reception of the Gospel of Jesus Christ according to Acts 16:19–24.

3. How can you explain Acts 16:25 considering the disciples' misery? Can it be explained with St. Paul's words in Philippians 4:7? What is "peace"?

4. Compare and contrast the world's solution to problems with the Lord's solution (Acts 16:27, 31). What response follows according to Acts 16:34?

5. Compare and contrast the washing the jailer provided for the disciples with the washing the jailer and his household received through Holy Baptism (Acts 16:33).

Connect

Jealousy, hatred, and persecution come from the world. All people are sinful from birth, separated from God by nature, and hostile toward the Law and the Gospel. Humankind opposes the Law because it shows our failures and inability to save ourselves. We reject the Gospel because we feel confident of our strength and achievement before God, though in fact we are "dead in transgressions and sins" (Ephesians 2:1). But God sends His Word of Law and Gospel, of judgment and grace, to all people. In mercy He calls us by the Gospel to faith, and in Christ we have the assurance of forgiveness and eternal life. This Good News is the "power of God for the salvation of everyone who believes: first for the Jew, then for the Gentile" (Romans 1:16).

1. Describe a time when you failed to carry out some important responsibility. Compare and contrast your reaction with that of the jailer (Acts 16:27). Did someone help you work through your sense

of failure? How does the Good News of Jesus help us and others to deal with guilt we experience over mistakes we've made?

2. How might you use the story of the jailer of Philippi as a reason for baptizing infants (note also other households being baptized, such as Acts 11:14; 16:15; 18:8)?

3. What things did you learn from Paul and Silas's experience in prison that might help you the next time you encounter a difficult time in life?

Vision

Family Connection

1. Discuss "joy." Have each member of the family draw a picture expressing their joy.

2. Ask, "How can we continue to experience joy even as we face a difficult time?" Review the story of Paul and Silas in jail. Ask, "What gave Paul and Silas joy even as they faced hardships?"

3. Develop "joy" cards together as a family to send to those who might be experiencing troubles and hardships in their lives. Include Philippians 4:4–9 on the card.

4. Read Philippians 4:4–9 every day for devotions. Have family members tell about things during the day that provided them joy.

Personal Reflection

1. Examine the reason for St. Paul's joy by reading Philippians 4:4–9. Concentrate on the things that are good in your life (v. 8),

especially your salvation, and give thanks.

2. Take out your baptismal certificate and read it. Review the blessings of Baptism according to Martin Luther in his Small Catechism.

3. If there is someone you work with or associate with who doesn't know you're a Christian, plan to share your faith with him/her.

Closing Worship

Pray the following prayer:

Lord God, send us out to be Your witnesses, who boldly demonstrate who we are and to whom we belong. In Jesus' name. Amen.

Adult Leaders Guide

Session 1

Jesus Provides for Us

(Matthew 14:14–21; Luke 10:25–37)

Focus

Theme: Our Greatest Need

Law/Gospel Focus

Read aloud or invite a volunteer to read aloud the Law/Gospel Focus.

Objectives

Invite volunteers to read aloud each of the objectives for this session.

Opening Worship

Speak together the First Article of the Apostles' Creed and Luther's explanation.

Introduction

1. Answers will vary.

2. Answers will vary. Sometime in our pursuit of other needs we may neglect or ignore our greatest need—forgiveness of sins and eternal life.

3. Answers will vary. Faith strengthened by the power of the Holy Spirit working through the Gospel enables and empowers us to love God and our neighbor.

Read aloud the closing paragraph.

Inform

Reading the Text

Read aloud Matthew 14:14–21 and Luke 10:25–37. Then read aloud or invite volunteers to read aloud the commentary in the Study Guide. If time is short, you may wish to summarize the major facts covered in the commentary or ask a participant to do so.

Discussing the Text

1. Jesus demonstrated His concern for the physical needs of people by healing their illnesses and feeding the crowds. This is important for us to know because we too have physical needs. Jesus cares about our physical needs and promises to provide all that we need to sustain our life.

2. Jesus feeds spiritually hungry people with His words of life.

3. In the Lord's Supper Jesus provides us His body and His blood in, with, and under common elements—bread and wine. Through faith we receive the forgiveness of sins through this heavenly meal.

4. Your neighbor is anyone you encounter. "Neighbor" is not determined by where you live.

5. Jesus gives up His life for those who from birth have been His enemies—all sinners. Jesus receives the punishment His enemies deserved so that they might enjoy the blessings of forgiveness of sins and eternal life.

Connect

Read aloud the paragraphs. Then discuss the questions that follow.

1. We at times neglect that which God provides to meet our spiritual need—His Word and Sacraments. Opportunities for Bible study, devotions, and worship are often crowded out of our lives by other things.

2. God continues to offer you love and forgiveness through faith in Jesus, even as we fail to "fear, love, and trust" in Him above all things. God is eager to forgive repentant sinners.

3. Answers will vary. As we demonstrate the joy and peace that only Jesus can give, we share with our neighbors God's love for us in Christ.

4. God's love for us in Christ Jesus motivates and empowers us to "Go and do likewise."

5. Provide participants time to write a prayer of thanksgiving to God for all of the physical and spiritual blessings He provides in our lives. Remind participants that volunteers will be invited to share their prayers of thanksgiving during closing worship.

Vision

To Do This Week

Urge participants to complete one or more of the suggested activities during the coming week.

Closing Worship

Invite volunteers to pray aloud the prayers of thanksgiving they wrote earlier.

For Next Week

Urge participants to read the assigned Scripture lessons for the next session.

Session 2

Jesus Gives Us the Lord's Supper

Luke 22:7–38

Focus

Theme: Dining at Its Best!

Read aloud the theme verse.

Law/Gospel Focus

Invite a volunteer to read aloud the Law/Gospel Focus.

Objectives

Invite a volunteer to read aloud each of the objectives for this session.

Opening Worship

Read responsively the dialogue-prayer based on Luke 22:19–20.

Introduction

Invite volunteers to read aloud the introduction. Then discuss the questions that follow.

1. At the beginning of most worship services there is confession and absolution. Upon confessing our sins, the pastor pronounces absolution by the command of Jesus Christ. In the Lord's Supper we receive the body and blood of Jesus for the forgiveness of sins. It is like "dessert." It is a very intimate way for God to convey His love to us. Through the very personal eating and drinking, we receive His forgiveness, faith-strengthening power, and the assurance of eternal life.

2. The Lord's Supper assures us "the best is yet to come" by giving us forgiveness. Martin Luther reminds us that where there is forgiveness of sins, there is also life and eternal salvation.

120

3. The Lord's Supper far exceeds any comparison with any earthly food, including any imaginable dessert; however, we do recognize some similarities. Desserts are savored and enjoyed. Holy Communion also is savored and enjoyed.

Inform

Reading the Text

Read aloud or invite volunteers to read aloud Luke 22:7–38. Then invite volunteers to read aloud the commentary.

Discussing the Text

1. There are many similarities between the Passover of the Old Testament and the Lord's Supper of the New Testament. A few of these similarities include the following: (a) "bread ... without yeast" (Exodus 12:18; Luke 22:19); (b) blood (Exodus 12:22; Luke 22:20; Matthew 26:28); (c) a passing over of the angel of death (Exodus 12:23; Matthew 26:28); (d) examination (Exodus 12:26; 1 Corinthians 11:28); (e) the sacrifice of a lamb (Exodus 12:21; 1 Corinthians 5:7); (f) deliverance, forgiveness, and redemption (Exodus 12:31–32; Matthew 26:28).

2. Luke 22:61 was fulfilled upon the sacrifice of the perfect "Passover lamb" (1 Corinthians 5:7; Isaiah 53:7; John 1:29). Jesus' sacrifice fulfilled perfectly the Passover promise and purpose. Through His perfect obedience and willing sacrifice the kingdom of God would come to a world fractured by sin and hostility.

3. We believe that in, with, and under the bread and wine Christ gives us His true body and blood. Jesus clearly says, "This is My body. ... This is My blood" (Matthew 26:26, 28). St. Paul reminds us that the bread and wine are in communion, or participation, in the body and blood of Christ (1 Corinthians 10:16).

Connect

Read aloud the paragraphs. Then discuss the questions that follow. If your class is large, you may wish to divide the class into small groups to discuss the questions. This will give all participants an opportunity to share.

1. Answers will vary.

2. Though both give absolute and total forgiveness, the Lord's Supper is a very personal way of bringing that forgiveness to each person. It is an intimate way of receiving forgiveness. This forgiveness is "for you" (1 Corinthians 11:24), given as you eat the very body and blood of the Savior.

3. Answers will vary.

4. Different congregations within The Lutheran Church—Missouri Synod offer Holy Communion at different times in a child's life. Some churches have begun to instruct children in the meaning of Holy Communion before they reach adolescence and, therefore, offer Communion at a much earlier age than 12–14. Whatever the congregation's policy, it is important that every communicant properly examine himself by asking, (1) Am I a Christian? (2) Am I being honest with myself and with God about my life? Do I repent of my sins, and do I really want God's help to change and grow? (3) Do I understand that in the Sacrament I receive more than just bread and wine? Christ Himself offers His body and blood as a visible assurance of God's grace and forgiveness.

Vision

Urge participants to complete one or more of the activities before the next session.

Closing Worship

Lead the class in the closing hymn.

For Next Week

Assign the Scripture lesson that will be studied in the next session: Luke 22:39–46.

Session 3

Jesus Prays in Gethsemane

Luke 22:39–46

Focus

Theme: Intimate Communication

Read aloud the theme verse.

Law/Gospel Focus

Invite a volunteer to read aloud the Law/Gospel Focus.

Objectives

Invite volunteers to read aloud each of the objectives for this session.

Opening Worship

Read responsively the dialogue-prayer based on Luke 22:39–46.

Introduction

Ask participants to discuss the questions. Answers will vary. Read the closing paragraph of this section aloud.

Inform

Reading the Text

Read aloud or invite volunteers to read aloud Luke 22:39–46. Then invite volunteers to read aloud the commentary.

Discussing the Text

1. We can bring our anxieties and troubles to the Lord, just as Jesus Himself did. When we struggle over doing His will, we can

come to Him in prayer. It isn't that God doesn't know what we're already experiencing; He does. However, in praying we lay our burdens before God, confident that He will comfort, encourage, and respond. Jesus agonized to the point that "His sweat was like drops of blood falling to the ground" (Luke 22:44); nevertheless, when He had finished praying to God, He was ready to bear the full load of people's sins.

2. The "cup" in Luke 22:42 refers to God's judgment, God's wrath. God's wrath and judgment are often compared to becoming drunk with wine (Isaiah 51:17). When reference is made to "drink of the cup," as it is in Matthew 20:22, it refers to suffering (Matthew 26:39).

3. Although Jesus experienced deep anguish over the suffering and death that He would experience, He demonstrated trust in His Father, knowing that whatever would occur, God would use it for good. The good in this case would be the forgiveness of sins and eternal life Jesus would earn for all people.

4. Each time Jesus returned to His disciples He found them sleeping (Luke 22:45). (a) Most of us would try our hardest to stay awake if a loved one was dying; however, we need to understand the disciples were still not really cognizant of everything that would happen to the Lord. Though they had heard Jesus say He would have to die, even Peter could not quite comprehend it. (b) Many things contributed to the disciples' sleepiness: anxiety, meetings that lasted long into the night, worry, etc. Accept all responses. (c) Some of the signs of spiritual sleepiness include staying away from church, not attending the Lord's Supper, seldom praying, not attending Bible study, etc. Whenever people remove themselves from the faith-strengthening power God provides through His means of grace, they jeopardize their spiritual relationship with the Lord; they become less able to resist the temptations of their sinful self, the world, and Satan. The signs of a congregation drifting into spiritual slumber might include poor attendance in worship and Bible study or an emphasis on the business of the congregation to the exclusion of an emphasis on Word and Sacrament.

Connect

Read aloud the paragraphs. Then discuss the questions that follow. If your class is large, you may wish to divide the class into small groups to discuss the questions. This will give all participants an opportunity to share.

1. Answers will vary. You would be witnessing to your friend or loved one your faith-reliance upon God and your trust in Him to answer prayer.

2. Answers will vary.

3. Answers will vary.

4. If there is any comfort in the fact that Jesus went through extreme anguish, it is that He understands the anguish we go through: "For we do not have a high priest who is unable to sympathize with our weaknesses, but we have one who has been tempted in every way, just as we are—yet was without sin. Let us then approach the throne of grace with confidence, so that we may receive mercy and find grace to help us in our time of need" (Hebrews 4:15–16).

Vision

Urge participants to complete one or more of the activities before the next session.

Closing Worship

Pray together the prayer.

For Next Week

Assign the Scripture lessons that will be studied during the next session: Luke 22:24–35, 54–62; 15:1–3, 11–32.

Session 4

Peter Denies Jesus

(Luke 22:24–35, 54–62; 15:1–3, 11–32)

Focus

Theme: Our Faithlessness, His Faithfulness

Read aloud the theme verse.

Law/Gospel Focus

Invite a volunteer to read aloud the Law/Gospel Focus.

Objectives

Invite volunteers to read aloud each of the objectives for this session.

Opening Worship

Read responsively the dialogue-prayer based on Luke 22:24–25, 54–62; 15:1–3, 11–32.

Introduction

Ask a volunteer to read aloud the story of the seminarian. Then discuss the questions that follow.

1–2. Answers will vary.

Then read aloud the closing paragraph.

Inform

Reading the Text

Read aloud or invite volunteers to read aloud Luke 22:24–35, 54–62; 15:1–3, 11–32. Then invite volunteers to read aloud the commentary.

Discussing the Text

1. Jesus Christ reversed the ways and values of the world by showing that real greatness in the kingdom is not measured by power and prestige, but by humility, service, and sacrifice. Jesus is exemplary of such service: "I am among you as one who serves" (Luke 22:27). He served by giving His life on the cross. Normally, foot-washing was done only by the hired hands. Jesus, however, did it for His disciples, indicating His willingness to be their servant.

2. The disciples did more than just walk away from Jesus after He was betrayed and arrested. Mark reminds us that they "fled" (Mark 14:50). They wanted out, and they got out as fast as they could, including Peter and John, two of Jesus' favorite disciples. Out of curiosity, Peter followed at a distance.

3. The look of Jesus must have been one of great disappointment, even though He had predicted it would happen (Luke 22:34). Jesus faced isolation from His disciples and ultimately, as He would die on the cross, isolation from God. Jesus saw that even one of His favorite disciples had forsaken Him. Peter had betrayed a dear Friend, one he promised he would never turn his back on. His look must have been one of shame and great guilt. Could he do anything but cry (Luke 22:62)?

4. Both Peter and Judas betrayed Jesus. Peter confessed his sins and received the grace of God in Jesus and was forgiven. Judas despaired and committed suicide.

Connect

Read aloud the paragraphs. Then discuss the questions that follow. If your class is large, you may wish to divide the class into small groups to discuss the questions. This will give all participants an opportunity to share.

1. Answers will vary.

2. Answers will vary.

3. Temporal adversaries we do battle with include hunger, illness, hardship, persecution, poverty, physical danger, and death itself; spiritual powers include evil angels, demons, and "the rulers … the authorities … the powers of this dark world and against the

spiritual forces of evil in the heavenly realms"(Ephesians 6:12). The promise is that "in all these things we are more than conquerors through Him who loved us" (Romans 8:37).

Vision

Urge participants to complete one or more of the activities before the next session.

Closing Worship

Sing or read aloud the hymn "I Am Trusting You, Lord Jesus."

For Next Week

Assign the Scripture lesson that will be studied in the next session: Luke 22:66–23:25.

Session 5

Pilate Condemns Jesus

(Luke 22:66–23:25)

Focus

Theme: Condemnation for Jesus; Freedom for Us

Read aloud the theme.

Law/Gospel Focus

Invite a volunteer to read aloud the Law/Gospel Focus.

Objectives

Invite volunteers to read aloud each of the objectives for this session.

Opening Worship

Read the dialogue-prayer responsively.

Introduction

Ask the participants to think about the story of the man who sacrificed himself to save a boy. Then discuss the questions that follow.

1. Yes, or they might have said, "And to think we chose him over the life of Jesus."

2. Jesus Christ willingly threw Himself before His enemies and died on the cross so that we might be saved, and yet we are so much like the little boy in the story. Though we have been redeemed by the precious blood of Jesus Christ, we continue to sin daily.

3. Jesus was willing to trade His innocence for our guilt for one reason and one reason only—He loved us. There is nothing logical about why He did what He did. His love is incomprehensible. "Oh,

the depth of the riches of the wisdom and knowledge of God! How unsearchable His judgments, and His paths beyond tracing out!" (Romans 11:33).

Inform

Reading the Text

Read aloud or invite volunteers to read aloud Luke 22:66–23:25. Then invite volunteers to read aloud the rather lengthy commentary.

Discussing the Text

1. The charges brought against Jesus varied. The leaders actually changed the charges during the course of the trial, from religious blasphemy to civil insurrection. They accused Him of that which was needed to get rid of Him. (a) Luke 22:67–70—the elders and priests in these verses accused Jesus of calling Himself the Christ. To be so brazen as to call oneself God's own Son was too much for them. This was blasphemy. (b) Luke 23:3—before Pilate the elders and priests changed their accusation. They knew that it would be treason for Jesus to call Himself "the king of the Jews," and so they led Him into saying this about Himself. (c) Luke 23:5—when the charge that He said He was the "king of the Jews" didn't work, the people shouted that He was a troublemaker and was causing a great deal of commotion, stirring people up in the city and elsewhere.

2. "Then Herod and his soldiers ridiculed and mocked Him" (Luke 23:11). It may have been common to go along with the commander, following their cues from him as far as what they should do, even regarding their taunts! Herod's soldiers do basically what Pilate's soldiers did.

3. When Jesus said He was the "king of the Jews," He, of course, meant that He was the promised Savior of the Jews, the one who would be proclaimed "King of kings" by all one day in heaven (Revelation 19:16). Pilate and the religious leaders thought "king of the Jews" was a political and social statement.

4. After Pilate recognizes Jesus is not guilty of the charges brought against Him, He does three things: (1) Luke 23:7—he

attempts to remove himself from the case by turning Jesus over to Herod, who happens to be in town; (2) Mark 15:5–11—he takes advantage of the Passover amnesty program, which allows him to release one criminal. He asks if they want Barabbas, a noted criminal, released, or Jesus! The crowd chooses Barabbas. (3) Matthew 27:24–25—he washes his hands as a symbol of his innocence!

Connect

Read aloud the paragraphs. Then discuss the questions that follow. If your class is large, you may wish to divide the class into small groups. This will give all participants an opportunity to share.

1. Answers will vary.
2. Answers will vary.
3. Barabbas represents all of us (the sinner, the ungodly—the truly and recognizably guilty). The substitution of the sinless Lamb of God for the convicted thief and murderer was a graphic demonstration of what the death of Jesus Christ on the cross was about to do for the whole human race. He who knew no sin was about to pay the price for the guilty ones who knew no holiness: His life for ours, His blood as the price for our freedom. His death for ours, so that with Paul we may say, "I have been crucified with Christ and I no longer live, but Christ lives in me. The life I live in the body, I live by faith in the Son of God, who loved me and gave Himself for me" (Galatians 2:20).

Vision

Urge participants to complete one or more of the activities before the next session.

Closing Worship

Sing or speak aloud the stanzas of "Chief of Sinners Though I Be."

For Next Week

Assign the Scripture lesson that will be discussed in the next session: Luke 19:28–44; 23:26–56.

Session 6

Jesus Is Put to Death

(Luke 19:28–44; 23:26–56.)

Focus

Theme: The Day Time Divided

Read aloud the theme verse.

Law/Gospel Focus

Invite a volunteer to read aloud the Law/Gospel Focus.

Objectives

Invite volunteers to read aloud each of the objectives for this session.

Opening Worship

Read responsively the dialogue-prayer.

Introduction

1. Many events that occur can change the course of history and the lives of people. Catastrophes, natural disasters, wars, reconciliation, etc., can all change the lives of people, and in so doing change the course of history.

2. The death of Jesus literally changed the world. Today there are millions of Christians throughout the world who subscribe to the basic teachings of Christianity, beginning with the death and resurrection of Jesus Christ. All other world religions speak of works-righteousness. Christianity speaks of salvation that is not earned but bestowed as a gift through Jesus' death and resurrection. Jesus finished paying for humanity's sins, though, unfortunately, many still attempt to work out their own salvation through good works. His death has certainly changed most of us, or we

would not be in this Bible class today. We could say, "If there was no death of Jesus or His resurrection, everything we believe would be useless."

3. Good Friday was "good" for us in every way. Jesus took upon Himself our punishment, the punishment we deserved because of our sin.

Inform

Reading the Text

Read aloud or invite volunteers to read aloud Luke 23:26–56. Then invite volunteers to read aloud the commentary.

Discussing the Text

1. Jesus warns them that there would be a great deal of weeping in the future. Forty years later the Romans besieged the city of Jerusalem and destroyed the temple.

2. It is important to remember that Jesus' love and forgiveness of His enemies had nothing to do with anything they did. His forgiveness was unconditional. Remember, we are saved "by grace … through faith—and this not from [our]selves, it is the gift of God" (Ephesians 2:8–9). We "were still sinners," and yet "Christ died for us" (Romans 5:8). Jesus' forgiveness for our sins is unconditional. We have done and can do nothing to earn it.

3. The law of life is based on the law of retribution: "Eye for eye, and tooth for tooth" (Exodus 21:24; Matthew 5:38) or "A man reaps what he sows" (Galatians 6:7). (a) Jesus did not get what He deserved. He was without sin, but He took our sin upon Himself to pay the price we should have received, death itself. (b) The first criminal basically got what he deserved—death itself, eternal death. (c) The second criminal got eternal life, the same that we get, and just as he did not deserve such a gift, so we do not. Yet through the life, death, and resurrection of Jesus Christ, the gift is ours.

4. Christ's death would bring about the most dramatic, earth-shattering experiences ever to take place in recorded history. He would literally turn the world upside down. The events during His death are a prelude to what would result because of His death. The

curtain dividing the Holy Place and the Most Holy Place in the temple was torn in two because it was no longer necessary. Now God's people no longer needed a high priest to make atonement for their sins. The atonement had taken place, once for all, through Jesus' death. Now we can go before God confidently "in full assurance of faith" (Hebrews 10:22).

Connect

Read aloud the paragraphs. Then discuss the questions that follow. If your class is large, you may wish to divide the class into small groups. This will give all participants an opportunity to share.

1. In Exodus 21:23–25, God said to Israel, "But if there is serious injury, you are to take life for life, eye for eye, tooth for tooth, hand for hand, foot for foot, burn for burn, wound for wound, bruise for bruise." In Deuteronomy 19:18–21, God said to Israel, "The judges must make a thorough investigation, and if the witness proves to be a liar, giving false testimony against his brother, then do to him as he intended to do to his brother. You must purge the evil from among you. The rest of the people will hear of this and be afraid, and never again will such an evil thing be done among you. Show no pity: life for life, eye for eye, tooth for tooth, hand for hand, foot for foot."

Considering the extreme nature of many capital crimes today, many people would not consider the electric chair "cruel and unusual punishment" (a term derived from Amendment VIII of the U.S. Constitution). Punishment will never and can never rid our world of crime. It only serves as a deterrent.

2. To "deny oneself" means to cease to make oneself the object of one's life and actions. It means Christ replaces our own selfishness. Such denial may even mean suffering and dying for Christ's sake. In the least, it means facing taunts and ridicule for often subscribing to things that are not "politically correct."

3. Answers will vary.

4. Answers will vary. Even at a very early age, children need to hear that Jesus died for their sins. As they grow older, they need to hear the entire story, including the graphic details included in the crucifixion account.

5. St. Paul said it well: "And if Christ has not been raised, our preaching is useless and so is your faith. ... But Christ has indeed been raised from the dead, the first fruits of those who have fallen asleep" (1 Corinthians 15:14, 20). If Christ had not been raised, we would still be in our sins. We believe that through living a perfect life, Jesus did for us what we could not do (Galatians 4:4–5). He suffered and died for us because the wages of our sin is death (Romans 6:23). He paid the price for our sinfulness, and through His rising from the dead, we can be assured that His death was sufficient payment for our sins.

Vision

Urge participants to complete one or more of the activities before the next session.

Closing Worship

Pray the prayer.

For Next Week

Assign the Scripture lesson that will be studied in the next session: Luke 24:1–11; Matthew 28:1-10; and 1 Corinthians 15:1-11.

Session 7

Jesus Rises from the Dead

(Luke 24:1–11; Matthew 28:1-10;
1 Corinthians 15:1-11)

Focus

Theme: The Central Doctrine of Christianity

Read aloud the theme verse.

Law/Gospel Focus

Invite a volunteer to read aloud the Law/Gospel Focus.

Objectives

Invite volunteers to read aloud each of the objectives for this session.

Opening Worship

Read responsively the dialogue-prayer.

Introduction

Ask participants to think about the way people celebrated VE Day. Then discuss the questions that follow.

1. On May 8, 1945, Germany surrendered and the war in Europe was over. Though many never took part in the actual combat, they claimed the victory because they were citizens of one of the countries that allied against Germany.

2. The Good News is that we didn't do anything in fighting the war against sin, death, and the power of the devil—but we won! How? Through Jesus Christ's victory. St. Paul reminds us that through Holy Baptism we are "buried with Him ... in order that, just as Christ was raised from the dead through the glory of the Father, we too may live a new life. If we have been united with Him like this in His death, we will certainly also be united with

Him in His resurrection" (Romans 6:1–5). When He won, *we won*! And we did nothing! In fact, we were the enemy.

Inform

Reading the Text

Read aloud or invite volunteers to read aloud Luke 24:1–11; Matthew 28:1-10; and 1 Corinthians 15:1-11. Then invite volunteers to read aloud the commentary.

Discussing the Text

1. Jesus' tomb was sealed by Pilate's authority because the chief priests and Pharisees had told Pilate that the "deceiver" (their term for Jesus) had said, "After three days I will rise again." They thought the disciples would steal the body and then tell the people Jesus had risen from the dead. Pilate, therefore, ordered a special seal to be placed on the stone covering the grave and sent soldiers to guard the grave (Matthew 27:62–66).

2. There was definite physical evidence of Jesus' resurrection: (1) the stone had been rolled away; (2) the body was missing; (3) the grave clothes were lying on the slab where the body had been laid. We must not be too judgmental of the doubt that the main characters of the resurrection displayed. After all, from their perspective, dead people didn't normally come back to life.

3. (a) The angels and Jesus asked "Why are you crying?" because Jesus was alive (John 20:13, 15). There was no need for Mary to weep. (b) It was not until Jesus said her name, "Mary," that she knew and recognized Him (John 20:16). (c) Many of us would have reacted the way Mary did. We would have undoubtedly embraced Him.

4. Christ's life, death, and resurrection are essential for salvation. (a) His perfect life did for us what we were unable to do, fulfill the Law: "God sent His Son, born of a woman, born under law, to redeem those under law, that we might receive the full rights of sons" (Galatians 4:4–5). (b) Jesus' death paid the price for our sins—death itself: "Christ died for our sins" (1 Corinthians 15:3). (c) His resurrection assures us that Jesus had paid the price for our

137

sins. His death was sufficient payment: "And if Christ has not been raised, your faith is futile; you are still in your sins" (1 Corinthians 15:17).

Connect

Read aloud the paragraphs. Then discuss the questions that follow. If your class is large, you may wish to divide the class into small groups to discuss the questions. This will give all participants an opportunity to share.

1. Suicide is often the result of hopelessness. The resurrection gives hope. It gives people a tomorrow, a promise of eternal life through the forgiveness earned by the life, death, and resurrection of Jesus Christ.

2. The resurrection of Jesus Christ assures us that we do not have to fear death, the power of sin, or Satan. His victory is our victory over all three.

3 (a) The price of my salvation was paid by Jesus Christ. Because of His life, death, and resurrection, I will live with Him in eternity. (b) Faith in Jesus Christ is the only way of salvation for all people.

4. True. The resurrection was promised by Jesus Christ. We can be assured; He keeps His promises, all of them.

Vision

Urge participants to complete one or more of the activities before the next session.

Closing Worship

Sing or read aloud the first stanza of "Jesus Lives! The Victory's Won."

For Next Week

Assign the Scripture lesson that will be studied during the next session: John 21.

Session 8

Jesus Appears at the Sea of Galilee

(John 21)

Focus

Theme: After the Resurrection

Read aloud the theme.

Law/Gospel Focus

Invite a volunteer to read aloud the Law/Gospel Focus.

Objectives

Invite volunteers to read aloud each of the objectives for this session.

Opening Worship

Read responsively the dialogue-prayer.

Introduction

Read aloud the story of the Easter pageant. Then discuss the questions that follow.

1. The burly man sought revenge. Jesus came not "to condemn the world, but to save the world" (John 3:17). After the resurrection Jesus assured the world that His life, death, and resurrection had paid the price we owed because of our sin—death itself.

2. Answers will vary.

3. Answers will vary.

Inform

Reading the Text

Read aloud or invite volunteers to read aloud John 21. Then invite volunteers to read aloud the commentary.

Discussing the Text

1. In both accounts Jesus visited the fishermen and performed a miracle—a great catch of fish. After the first miracle He reminded Peter that from this point on he would "catch men," meaning he would catch people for Jesus by sharing the Gospel. In the second miracle the disciples were fishing, and once again they caught a great catch of fish upon following Jesus' orders. Even though Peter had been disobedient, Jesus came to restore him and remind him that his discipleship would continue (John 21:7).

2. When Jesus asked the question, "Friends, haven't you any fish?" He was saying to them, "Hey, I'm interested in your lives, including something as simple as fishing." The resurrection is not just for the hereafter, it is for today as well. Jesus lives now! Present tense. He is concerned about every aspect of our lives.

3. Jesus instructed His disciples to "throw your net on the right side of the boat and you will find some [fish]" (John 21:6). Once they did, they were unable to haul the net in because of the large number of fish. We find it difficult at times to be God-directed because our sinful nature tempts us to be self-directed.

4. Jesus predicted that Peter would die a martyr's death. Tradition tells us that Peter was crucified upside down.

Connect

Read aloud the paragraphs. Then discuss the questions that follow. If your class is large, you may wish to divide the class into small groups to discuss the questions. This will give all participants an opportunity to share.

1. Answers will vary.

2. Answers will vary.

3. Answers will vary. No doubt Jesus would say, "I am with you always."

4. Jeremiah 31:33–34 shares the comforting truth, "For I will forgive their wickedness and will remember their sins no more." Like all other promises, God keeps this one.

Vision

Urge participants to complete one or more of the activities before the next session.

Closing Worship

Sing or read aloud "He's Risen, He's Risen."

For Next Week

Assign the Scripture lesson that will be studied in the next session: Acts 9:1–20.

Session 9

Saul Becomes a Christian

(Acts 9:1–20)

Focus

Theme: God's Love for All Humanity

Read aloud the theme.

Law/Gospel Focus

Invite a volunteer to read aloud the Law/Gospel Focus.

Objectives

Invite volunteers to read aloud each of the objectives for this session.

Opening Worship

Read responsively the dialogue-prayer based on Romans 7:18–25.

Introduction

Read aloud the introductory section. Then discuss the questions.

1. Answers will vary.
2. Answers will vary.
3. Answers will vary.

Inform

Reading the Text

Read aloud or invite volunteers to read aloud Acts 9:1–20. Then invite volunteers to read aloud the commentary.

Discussing the Text

1. Many different things strike us as we read about Paul's conversion. Certainly, to many of us the fact that God chose one who was actually murdering His followers shows His limitless mercy and goodness.

2. The early Christians were referred to as "the Way" (Acts 9:2). It was a primitive Jewish-Christian idiom denoting early Christians. Jesus said, "I am the way," meaning He is the only way to the Father (John 14:6). As God's people we are empowered by Jesus' love to show others that Jesus is the only way to the Father.

3. Saul was temporarily blinded in his conversion. He could not see for three days (Acts 9:9). After Ananias placed his hands upon him, Saul could see again (Acts 9:18). When John announced that the "Word" had become flesh, he also announced that this Word was to be "the light of men" (John 1:4). Jesus makes it clear that He is the Light of the world: "I am the light of the world. Whoever follows Me will never walk in darkness, but will have the light of life" (John 8:12).

4. The Lord was gracious indeed in coming to Saul and embracing him in love and forgiveness. It seems only appropriate that someone who is known as "one who is gracious" bring God's graciousness to Saul (Acts 9:17–19).

5. Although Saul's conversion was quite different than ours, Scripture is clear that God chooses us; we do not choose Him (John 15:16). The story of Paul's conversion certainly illustrates this truth.

Connect

Read aloud the paragraphs. Then discuss the questions that follow. If your class is large, you may wish to divide into small groups to discuss the questions. This will give all participants an opportunity to share.

1. Answers will vary.

2. Answers will vary.

3. Though St. Paul recognized and confessed that he was "the worst" of sinners, "Christ came into the world to save sinners" (1 Timothy 1:15).

4. Answers will vary. The Lord promises to strengthen our faith through His means of grace—Word and Sacraments. Through these means the Holy Spirit works to enable and empower us for lives of obedience to God.

Vision

Urge participants to complete one or more of the activities before the next session.

Closing Worship

Sing or speak aloud the stanzas of "Just as I Am."

For Next Week

Assign the Scripture lessons that will be discussed in the next session: Acts 9:21–31; 13:1–33.

Session 10

Paul Begins His Ministry

(Acts 9:21–31; 13:1–33)

Focus

Theme: Chosen Instruments

Read aloud the theme.

Law/Gospel Focus

Invite a volunteer to read aloud the Law/Gospel Focus.

Objectives

Invite volunteers to read aloud each of the objectives for this session.

Opening Worship

Read responsively the dialogue-prayer.

Introduction

Ask the participants to compare the conversion of the prisoner to Paul's conversion. Then discuss the questions that follow.

1. Many people feel that such "conversions" are only a con game. One must be careful not to suggest that all these conversions are a hoax. Some of them are very sincere and truly life-changing, similar to St. Paul's.

2. Many Christians would have been skeptical of St. Paul because they knew Paul (Saul) hated Christians and tried to eliminate them.

3. Answers will vary.

Inform

Reading the Text

Read aloud or invite volunteers to read aloud Acts 9:21–31; 13:1–33. Then allow volunteers to read aloud the commentary.

Discussing the Text

1. St. Paul was trained under Gamaliel, the most honored rabbi of the first century (Acts 22:3). He had been trained in the Old Testament scriptures! He knew all the promises given by the prophets. This equipped him well for the arguments by the Jews against Jesus being the promised Savior. Of course, Paul's conversion made him a believer and a witness to the Savior (Acts 9:1–9).

2. The listeners may have thought Paul was a spy—one who sought to capture more believers, as he had done before his conversion (Acts 9:21). As Saul "grew more and more powerful," it baffled the Jews, and they "conspired to kill him" (Acts 9:22–23). God protected Paul from harm by having his friends lower "him in a basket through an opening in the wall" (Acts 9:25).

3. The name *Barnabas* means "son of encouragement" (Acts 4:36). When the church was highly suspicious of Saul, Barnabas defended him against false accusations. He accepted Paul and believed that the Holy Spirit had indeed changed him.

4. The early Christians "were worshiping the Lord and fasting" when the Holy Spirit came and told them to send Barnabas and Saul out to be foreign missionaries (Acts 13:2). They then "placed their hands on them and sent them off" (Acts 13:3). We would also do well to spend time in worship and fasting before we do the work of the church. Too often our decisions are made without seeking God's guidance and will in His Word or with little or no prayer.

5. The first part of Paul's sermon consisted of historical information about the role God played in Israel's life and history (Acts 13:17–25). The second part of the sermon contained the wonderful Good News of salvation, ending with a wonderful invitation for all to believe and confess this Good News (Acts 13:26–41). In every sermon a pastor includes both Law and Gospel. The Law leads the listeners to confess their sins and recognize their need for

a Savior. The Gospel comforts them, assuring them that Jesus won their forgiveness through His death on the cross.

Connect

Read aloud the opening paragraphs. Then discuss the questions that follow. If your class is large, you may wish to divide the class into small groups to discuss the questions. This will give all participants an opportunity to share.

1. Answers will vary.

2. Answers will vary. Paul was involved in the stoning of Stephen.

3. Answers will vary.

4. We know the Holy Spirit speaks to us through the means of grace, Word and Sacraments. Because He does, it is important that we hear the Word of God often in worship, Bible study, and in our own private meditation. We respond in faith as we pray, praise, and give thanks to God.

5. Answers will vary.

Vision

Urge participants to complete one or more of the activities before the next session.

Closing Worship

Pray together the closing prayer.

For Next Week

Assign the Scripture lessons that will be studied in the next session: Acts 13:44–52; 16:1–5; and 2 Timothy 1:5–7; 3:14–16.

Session 11

Paul Preaches
to Jews and Gentiles

(Acts 13:44–52; 16:1–5; 2 Timothy 1:5–7; 3:14–16)

Focus

Theme: For All the People of the World

Read aloud the theme.

Law/Gospel Focus

Invite a volunteer to read aloud the Law/Gospel Focus.

Objectives

Invite volunteers to read aloud each of the objectives for this session.

Opening Worship

Read responsively the dialogue-prayer based on Romans 10:12–15.

Introduction

Ask participants to think about the story concerning Jesus. Then discuss the questions that follow.

1. Answers will vary.

2. We pray that our children and grandchildren will be in heaven with us; however, the truth of the matter is faith cannot be transferred from one person to the next like the ownership of a car. Faith is personal. Each person must believe. It is certainly our privilege and responsibility to share the Good News of salvation with our children and children's children, but no one has the ability or power to convert anyone. Only the Holy Spirit can and does accomplish this work.

3. Answers will vary.

Inform

Reading the Text

Read aloud or invite volunteers to read aloud Acts 13:44–52; 16:1–5; and 2 Timothy 1:5–7; 3:14–16. Then ask volunteers to read aloud the commentary.

Discussing the Text

1. Paul and the early apostles met with opposition from the Jews for one simple reason—jealousy. "When the Jews saw the crowds, they were filled with jealousy" (Acts 13:45a). Unfortunately, similar things happen too often in the church today.

2. Paul spoke the truth: "We had to speak the word of God to you first. Since you reject it and do not consider yourselves worthy of eternal life, we now turn to the Gentiles. For this is what the Lord has commanded us: 'I have made you a light for the Gentiles, that you may bring salvation to the ends of the earth.' " (Acts 13:46–47). The Jews had been a chosen people, set apart by God. For the Jews the words were Law, not Gospel. Change was occurring. God revealed to the Jewish people that He was the God of the Gentiles as well!

3. The word *appointed* means the Gentiles had actually been chosen to believe in Jesus Christ as Lord and Savior. They were chosen before eternity to believe, just as we were. St. Paul repeatedly makes this point throughout his epistles: "For those God foreknew He also predestined to be conformed to the likeness of His Son, that He might be the firstborn among many brothers. And those He predestined He also called; those He called, He also justified; those He justified, He also glorified" (Romans 8:29–30). Though Scripture speaks of predestination, meaning the choosing of those who believe, it does not speak of double predestination, meaning that He also chose some not to believe. Though one seems to follow the other logically, remember God does not think and reason as we do. Scripture clearly reveals that God desires no one to perish (2 Peter 3:9).

4. Timothy had become a believer at the feet of his mother, Eunice, and his grandmother, Lois. Both Lois and Eunice had been devout Jews who had received the Christian faith. "I have been reminded of your sincere faith, which first lived in your grandmother Lois and in your mother Eunice and, I am persuaded, now lives in you also" (2 Timothy 1:5). Timothy's father was a Gentile.

5. Timothy had learned the revealed truth of God from Scripture. He had learned that salvation came "through faith in Christ Jesus" (2 Timothy 3:15). However, through Scripture he had also learned how to live his life in practical ways. The Scriptures told him how to live so that he could "be thoroughly equipped for every good work" (2 Timothy 3:17).

Connect

Read aloud the paragraphs. Then discuss the questions that follow. If your class is large, you may wish to divide the class into small groups. This will give all participants an opportunity to share.

1. Tolerance of evil is itself evil! God wants us to speak the truth, even though it's difficult at times, but to speak it always with love (Ephesians 4:15). To truly love someone means to be bold enough to speak God's Word to them.

2. The doctrine of predestination is a study in and by itself; however, there are certain truths about predestination that are made known through the few verses studied today. (a) False. Predestination and foreknowledge are not the same things. He foreknew who would be predestined; however, He did not predestine on the basis of any foreknowledge (Romans 8:29). (b) True. Predestination is not logically understood by the human mind; however, that does not negate it's truthfulness. Because we do believe, we find great comfort in the fact that we have been chosen. (c) True. Predestination is another verification that salvation comes only by God's grace without any merit or worthiness on our part (Ephesians 2:8–9). (d) True. God does see His chosen with glorified bodies (Romans 8:30).

3. It is essential that all of Scripture is inspired, or "God-breathed," as St. Paul reminds us in 2 Timothy 3:16, because it is a reliable norm. If it was not God-inspired, it would be no different

than our own words or someone else's words. As parents, we can boldly state that the words we speak to our children are God's words and that they come with authority. The same is true when speaking to a friend about his/her wrongdoing.

4. Though modeling a Christian life is essential, it is also important that we share the words of salvation with them. Jesus made it clear that His words are "spirit and ... life" (John 6:63).

Vision

Urge participants to complete one or more of the activities before the next session.

Closing Worship

Partner participants and have them speak the blessing to one another.

For Next Week

Assign the Scripture lessons that will be studied in the next session: Acts 14:8–23 and 16:6–15.

Session 12

Paul Proclaims the Good News in Lystra, Derbe, Macedonia, and Philippi

(Acts 14:8–23 and 16:6–15)

Focus

Theme: Being Politically Incorrect for the Sake of the Gospel

Read aloud the theme.

Law/Gospel Focus

Invite a volunteer to read aloud the Law/Gospel Focus.

Objectives

Invite volunteers to read aloud each of the objectives for this session.

Opening Worship

Read responsively the dialogue-prayer based on Matthew 28:19–20.

Introduction

Read aloud the opening sentence. Then discuss the questions.

1. Answers will vary.

2. We live in a society that promotes individualism and alternative life choices and styles. To confront sin as sin is often considered politically incorrect.

3. When our concern for political correctness takes precedence over the truth found in God's Word, we risk negating the power and purpose of the Law. Without the Law there is little or no need

for the message of the Gospel—Jesus Christ came to earth to suffer and die for our sins.

Inform

Reading the Text

Read aloud or invite volunteers to read aloud Acts 14:8–18 and 16:6–15. Then invite volunteers to read aloud the commentary.

Discussing the Text

1. The secret to any healing is always "faith" (Acts 14:9). Paul saw the crippled man "had faith to be healed" and so Paul healed him (Acts 14:9). Repeatedly, forgiveness and physical healing were announced whenever faith was evident; consider the healing of the paralytic (Luke 5:20), the woman who anointed Jesus with oil (Luke 7:50), the woman who touched Jesus' cloak (Luke 8:48), and the leprous man (Luke 17:19).

2. After healing the lame man, the people announced, "The gods have come to visit us in the likeness of men." Barnabas and Paul were thought to be Jupiter and Mercury. The news was exciting. Immediately the people began to make plans to honor the men in the temple with great festivities. Needless to say, when Paul and Barnabas heard what was happening, they became very upset. Many might have taken advantage of the situation, accepted the praises of the people, and received whatever they wanted. However, Paul and Barnabas served the true God and had come to abolish this type of idolatry. David Koresh and other cult leaders program their followers to give them homage and honor.

3. The first sermon preached to this pagan audience contained the following truths: The living God is the one "who made heaven and earth and sea and everything in them" (Acts 14:15); God shows "kindness by giving ... rain from heaven and crops in their seasons, ... provides ... plenty of food and fills ... hearts with joy" (Acts 14:17). Paul begins with the truth of one God, who alone blesses all people with His gifts from heaven. He does not immediately proclaim Jesus as the Messiah and their Savior.

4. The first convert outside Palestine and Asia Minor was Lydia

(Acts 16:14–15). She sold the famed Thyatiran dyed purple cloth. Lydia was a Gentile who was a "worshiper of God," the God the Jews worshiped. The Lord opened her heart through the Word of God spoken by the apostles. Through the Spirit of God she confessed Jesus Christ as Lord, who alone provided salvation through His life, death, and resurrection. Only the Holy Spirit opens our hearts. He does this through the means of grace—Word and Sacraments.

Connect

Read aloud the paragraphs. Then discuss the questions that follow. If your class is large, you may wish to divide the class into small groups to discuss the questions. This will give all participants an opportunity to share.

1. Answers will vary. The Holy Spirit working through God's Word strengthens our faith, enabling us to face opposition courageously.

2. Answers will vary.

3. Answers will vary.

4. Answers will vary. All of our plans as God's children are predicated on God's will. As we trust in God, He guides and directs our lives.

Vision

Urge participants to complete one or more of the activities before the next session.

Closing Worship

Sing or read aloud the stanzas of "Fight the Good Fight."

For This Week

Assign the Scripture lesson that will be studied during the next session: Acts 16:16–40.

Session 13

Paul Proclaims the Good News to a Jailer

(Acts 16:16–40)

Focus

Theme: The "Jailhouse Rock"

Read aloud the theme.

Law/Gospel Focus

Invite a volunteer to read aloud the Law/Gospel Focus.

Objectives

Invite volunteers to read aloud each of the objectives for this session.

Opening Worship

Pray responsively the prayer.

Introduction

Ask participants to think about the role of prayer in their lives. Then discuss the questions.

1. Answers will vary.
2. Answers will vary.
3. Answers will vary.

Inform

Reading the Text

Read aloud or invite volunteers to read aloud Acts 16:16–40. Invite volunteers to read aloud the commentary.

Discussing the Text

1. The woman described in Acts 16:16–19 was a fortune-teller and diviner. She was a source of much profit to her owners. In many cities it is not difficult to find places where one can go to have one's fortune read. Once a client consults a fortune-teller, they are often led to believe that much more can be revealed in additional sessions. Today, besides fortune-telling, many businesses profit from sinful activity. Examples include abortion clinics and prostitution houses (such as those legalized in Nevada). Any opposition to these practices angers those who profit from the trade.

2. After being accused of disrupting the peace and teaching an illegal religion, they were stripped to the waist and whipped in the market square. Bleeding and half unconscious, they were cast into the innermost part of the prison, a dark, dismal place. There they were given over to a jailer who was responsible for guarding them and making sure they did not escape.

3. The disciples knew that despite their bleak situation, God was in control. He had not abandoned them. St. Paul defines the Christian's confidence in Philippians 4:7: "And the peace of God, which transcends all understanding, will guard your hearts and your minds in Christ Jesus." Peace comes from knowing and confessing God is in control.

4. The world can only promise despair and hopelessness: the jailer wanted to commit suicide (Acts 16:27). The Lord's solution—forgiveness through the life, death, and resurrection of Jesus Christ (Acts 16:31). Can anyone do anything other than respond with joy over such Good News (Acts 16:34)? Someone once said, "Joyless Christians are a contradiction."

5. The jailer washed physical wounds. The jailer was washed spiritually through Holy Baptism. As Paul reminds us, "He saved us, not because of righteous things we had done, but because of His mercy. He saved us through the washing of rebirth and renewal by the Holy Spirit, whom He poured out on us generously through Jesus Christ our Savior" (Titus 3:5–6).

Connect

Read aloud the paragraphs. Then discuss the questions that follow. If your class is large, you may wish to divide the class into small groups. This will give all participants an opportunity to share.

1. Answers will vary. The Good News of Jesus Christ provides us worth, even as we admit failure.

2. Once the adults in a household became believers and were baptized, so everyone in the household was baptized. This certainly included infants. Throughout the Book of Acts examples are given of entire households being baptized: Cornelius (11:4), Lydia (16:15), Crispus (18:8). God bestows the gift of faith to *all* people through Holy Baptism.

3. Answers will vary.

Vision

Urge participants to complete one or more of the activities before the next session.

Closing Worship

Pray together the prayer.

THE HAWK TEMPLE
AT TIERRA GRANDE